What Happens If…

NAVIGATING YOUR LIFE PATH

WITH A FINANCIAL GPS

SHEHNAZ HUSSAIN

B.Sc, B.Ed, CHS, CLU

ISBN-10: 1540304442

ISBN-13: 978-1540304445

DEDICATION

This book is dedicated to My son Zameer and granddaughter Aneesa, who give purpose to my life. And to my daughter Shaista…wherever you are and whatever you do, my love follows you.

ACKNOWLEDGMENTS

I want to acknowledge my family in South Africa and my family of friends in Canada and around the world, as well as all the people that have touched my life at any given time. I am a product of the love, teaching, guidance and wisdom received from each person in my life. Both the easy and the hard-learned lessons have made me who I am today and I am very grateful to all of you. My life has shown that it takes a global village to help a person unveil their potential.

As I write this, I realize there are so many people to be thankful for. My unending gratitude goes out especially to the many financial advisors who have worked with me over the years and to the women of GroYourBiz and UnitedSucces, who have become a vital community of support, as I venture forth on my own.

Finally, a special acknowledgement to Anne Toner Fung, who has guided me in bringing this work to fruition.

Thank you for reading.

FOREWORD

When I was in my late twenties, my father died. He was not an old man and I always thought he'd be around to watch his grandchildren grow up. Sometimes life has other plans for us. At that time, over twenty years ago, on top of shock and grief at his loss, I also faced the confusion of navigating our legal and taxation systems as the untried executor of his will. Frustrated by my lack of knowledge and desperate to make the best possible decisions to ensure the financial well-being of my disabled mother, I reached out to professionals for advice. That was my first experience with a financial advisor. The inestimable value I derived from that relationship led me to become a Certified Financial Planner (CFP), because no one should have to flounder in a sea of red-tape and acronyms while caught up in life's most painful realities. For ten years, I helped others navigate that sea.

Although life has taken me down many paths (from management consulting to academia), since those years in financial services, I have never forgotten what it meant to have someone in my corner, with the expertise I needed, at that pivotal moment in my life.

Last year, when I met Shehnaz Hussain across a boardroom table, I immediately recognized another purpose-driven financial advisor. I was intrigued when she said she wanted to write a book. A book that would show people what it's like to work with a good financial advisor: the kind of advisor who really gets to the heart of what matters to you and your family. I was even more intrigued when she explained that the book would also show novice advisors how to build a strong, ethical, client-centred practice.

It seemed like a tall order for one book!

Now, just over a year has passed, the book is written and I've been asked to contribute this foreword. I am delighted to discover that Shehnaz has woven the lessons she hopes to impart into a rich tapestry—the fictional tale of two very real people and their extended family. While recounting this compelling story, Shehnaz also reveals the thoughts and aspirations of the financial advisor who helps them sort through many personal and financial complexities. The story's multiple threads are skillfully woven into one coherent picture, capturing both the inner workings of a team-based financial and insurance practice and the challenges families face when the needs of multiple generations and wildly different perspectives collide.

Never forgetting that the objective of the book is to enlighten as well as entertain, Shehnaz concludes each chapter with key takeaways that summarize the most important messages for both clients and advisors, as illustrated by recent events in the narrative. For those who like to jot down notes and questions as they read, blank notes pages are also included at the end of each chapter. In short, she has crafted a book that allows the reader to explore as they prefer and to select their own way of journeying.

Since you are reading this foreword, you clearly have an interest in the topic of financial planning. If you simply want to learn about the thousands of financial products and services available in the market today, there is no shortage of information available (as one quick search on Google will demonstrate!).

If, however, you seek a deeper understanding of the process of working with a financial advisor, the potential scope of that relationship, and how specific financial products can be integrated with unique, individual needs—read this book. Whether you choose to focus on the storyline, the chapter-by-chapter learning opportunity, or the journaling and self-exploration this book facilitates, you will discover something of great value between these pages.

Anne Toner Fung, MBA CFP, CHRL
Executive Director, Innovation Guelph
Contributing Author, Citizen-Led Innovation for a New Economy
Kitchener, ON

CONTENTS

SHEHNAZ HUSSAIN

1. INTRODUCTION

Have you ever wondered how we managed to travel and successfully arrive at our destination, before the invention of the GPS? The most recent versions of these incredible devices even warn us of traffic jams and suggest alternate routes, all while automatically updating our arrival time!

Much like a GPS helps us navigate the chaos of today's roads, a financial advisor helps us navigate our financial journey. We decide on the destination and whether we want to take the fastest route or avoid the stress of the highway. Then, based on our goals and the parameters we set, our financial advisor identifies the most efficient route. More importantly, our financial advisor monitors the environment around us and responds to problems encountered along the way, continually updating the financial roadmap to suit our circumstances.

A GPS is not what makes travel possible, it just makes the process more efficient and much less prone to delay, distress and traffic gridlock. A good financial advisor offers the same performance advantage and peace of mind on your financial journey through life.

I have been an insurance and financial advisor for 16 years. Helping people successfully reach their desired financial destination, while protecting themselves and their loved ones—that is what I do!

You could say I'm a financial GPS!

With all the value this brings to my clients, I am still asked by friends and family (and even strangers) two very pointed questions!

How could you choose to be in sales?, and

Of all things to sell, why insurance?

These questions (and the tone they're usually delivered in!) always disturb me; because they clearly suggest there is something not quite admirable about either sales or insurance—and I fail to understand why.

Allow me to explain. First I'll tackle "why insurance?"

I started my career working for an organization that provided emergency monitors for people with limited mobility. You know, the pendant with the button the person pushes, saying "I've fallen and I can't get up!" As soon as the monitor is activated, someone is immediately dispatched to assist.

Providing a service that could save lives, which allowed the elderly and people with disabilities to live more safely in their own homes, was very satisfying to me. Until I realized that many of those who most needed the service, couldn't afford the $40 monthly monitoring fee. The more I saw potential customers (often widows on fixed incomes), reluctantly turn away from our service because of cost, the more concerned I became.

About that time, several people in my life experienced personal tragedy through the loss of a spouse. On top of the devastating grief of being left alone in their later years, they also faced the continuing burden of supporting themselves with limited financial resources.

Some of these people, my friends and family, subsequently faced years of living hand-to-mouth, because they just hadn't planned for this kind of life-shattering event.

It suddenly struck me that people I cared about were facing the same reality as those prospective customers, who couldn't afford an extra $40 monthly expense to help keep them safe.

Something was horribly wrong with that picture!

So, I started to investigate how it was that some people managed to be affluent throughout their lives, while others struggled to make ends meet.

There was no simple answer. In some cases, family money had been passed down and invested wisely. In others, business success had provided ample resources. But the most consistent factor I found was a habit of sound financial planning with a strong risk management component…in other words, savings and insurance.

The more I talked to people who had successfully weathered the same kind of storms my friends and family were struggling with, the clearer it became that insurance is one of the most effective ways to protect against the unexpected catastrophes we all face at one time or another in our lives.

In the course of my search for answers, I also discovered the many ways insurance can protect us from financial distress by providing income after an injury or with the diagnosis of a major illness. I was surprised to find how often insurance can help with finances while living, not just in the event of death. This was all new to me!

As for sales, it's simply about perspective. To me, a good sales person is someone who focuses on understanding the needs and wants of a client and then helping that client meet those needs and fulfill those wants.

That being the case, why do so many people have a negative impression of sales? Sadly, just as in any profession, not all sales people are caring salespeople. Some have their own self-serving agenda, and others simply lack the knowledge or training to function as a trusted advisor.

One of the reasons I'm writing this book is to help people recognize and understand the difference between an effective insurance and financial advisor and a salesperson whose priorities may not always align with their best interests – but I'm getting ahead of myself!

Back to addressing "why sales?" In a nutshell, without implementation, financial good intentions are about as useful as a trip without a destination. The best financial roadmap is just a bunch of paper sitting in a drawer (or bits and bytes stored on a computer), if those directions are never followed.

Finances, investments and insurance are complicated. Unless you are highly motivated to learn and able to pursue a lengthy course of self-study, you probably need the help of a financial professional when developing a financial plan and navigating the many options for implementing it. Given the way our financial industry is structured, that financial professional is most likely licensed to sell various financial products.

In other words, implementing your financial plan will likely involve working with one or more salespeople. This is true whether you work with a bank, a mutual fund company, a securities broker, an independent financial planner or an insurance advisor. Although you can find qualified financial planners who work on a fee-for-service basis, they are the minority and they are typically paid to prepare your plan, not to ensure that you implement it.

Unlike many people, I've never seen sales in a negative light. Every time my granddaughter, Aneesa, looks at me with her clear hazel eyes and convinces me that it would be good for both of us if we took a walk to the nearby playground, I know that those persuasive skills will serve her well in life. Besides, she is right, the walk does me good too and watching her play feeds my soul!

We are all sales people sometimes!

In my role as an advisor, it's my job to bring all my knowledge and skills to the table. Starting with the questioning and listening that allows me to understand a client's situation, what matters to them and what they want to accomplish. The first step is to achieve a comfortable level of trust between us. The next step is conducting research and applying my experience to identify solutions that will take them where they want to go.

It is also my responsibility to convince my clients to do what is necessary to reach the goals they have identified as important to them. Often this means confronting their greatest fears. Here are just a few of the "nightmare scenarios" I routinely help clients overcome.

- outliving the money

- dying before the children grow up

- becoming a "bag lady"

- being left alone with insufficient income

- becoming too ill to work

- being a burden on adult children

- ending up in a bad nursing home

In most cases, banishing these nightmares involves putting the right solutions in place to deal with the fallout when life takes a turn for the worse.

So, why sales? If helping people do what they need to do to protect who they love, get what they need, and do what they want in life is sales, then I am happy to be in sales.

The way I see it, if your doctor does everything possible to convince you to give up smoking and change your diet after a heart attack, because you say you want to be able to golf for another 20 years, you don't despise your doctor. If your personal trainer pushes you hard because you "must" get into your best suit before your only child's wedding, you don't claim the trainer is taking advantage of you.

In the same way, when a professional you turn to for help urges you to do what you need to do to accomplish an objective you have identified as important, she[1] is doing her job. The key is to find a knowledgeable, ethical and trustworthy professional, who understands your circumstances and has your best interests at heart. This book will help you do that. It will also help you understand the process you can expect to work through with a good financial advisor. Finally, it will illustrate effective financial strategies and how everyday people facing everyday challenges can use them to solve financial problems and protect their families from the unexpected. So, let's get started!

As you read this book, you will likely think about your own circumstances and ponder questions you would like to research or ask your own advisor about. To help you capture those thoughts and questions, we've provided a few blank pages at the end of chapters two through ten, where you can jot things down as you think of them.

Research shows that one of the best ways to provide information and have it be remembered is by sharing stories people can relate to.[2] Or, as they say in Missouri—show me! That's why you won't find a financial

---

[1] In the US, 35.5% of personal financial advisors are women (Bureau of Labor Statistics). In Canada, that number is slightly higher (Catalyst). Since both the author of this book and its fictional advisor are female, "she" is used when referencing professionals.
[2] Denise Lee, Jessica Simmons, Jennifer Drueen, Knowledge sharing in practice: applied storytelling and knowledge communities at NASA, Retrieved from http://www.inderscienceonline.com/doi/abs/10.1504/IJKL.2005.006258

planning textbook in the following chapters. Instead, you will meet Janet and Wasai: a married couple nearing retirement, who have many questions about their current financial situation…and many more about their future.

Although they are not actual people you might bump into at the grocery story, Janet and Wasai are very real. The situations they find themselves in and the challenges they face are all based on actual circumstances I have encountered with clients over the years. And the exploratory process they follow with their advisor is true-to-life, as are the solutions and strategies they choose to pursue.

Let's join Janet and Wasai as they get ready to visit a friend.

2. THE REFERRAL

Janet fidgeted with the buttons on the front of her blouse. She hated the way the fabric always gapped at the front, making her self-conscious. Looking over at her husband Wasai, she watched as he put on the same suit, shirt and tie he wore to every "dress up" event they had ever attended. Oh, if only it could be that simple!

Aside from feeling a brief sense of relief that everything still fit, Wasai gave little thought to what he was wearing. He was more concerned about making it through the afternoon. If Nancy's friends started getting weepy, he knew he'd have to find a place to hide. He looked up from knotting his tie. "It's been 6 months since John died. How is Nancy doing?"

"She sounds fine, but you know how reserved she is. Seems odd - after asking everyone to give her space these past few months, to have a 'drop-in' memorial." Janet carefully secured the front of her blouse from the inside with a safety pin, straightened out the fabric and glanced once more into the mirror. "I guess we'd better get going. Do you think this blouse looks okay?"

Muttering something non-committal, Wasai quickly headed for the front door, car keys in hand.

The drive to Nancy's house was brief and soon Janet and Wasai were swept into the brightly lit living room where they had enjoyed many pleasant evenings of conversation with Nancy and John, before he lost his battle with cancer. Wasai was happy to see that only a few people were still there. The informal drop-in format made it easy for people to visit briefly and then get back to their weekend errands and chores.

Stepping into the familiar space, Janet felt a rush of guilt as she realized how little contact she'd had with Nancy since John's funeral. And here they were, arriving late! Nancy had been so adamant about dealing with John's loss in solitude. It was always so hard to know whether people truly wanted privacy after a loss. But this was Nancy—independent, self-assured and able to handle anything. When Nancy asked for space, Janet didn't push back. She fell back on a heartfelt sympathy card with the standard "call me if I can help in any way" note. But Nancy hadn't called and the months just slid by.

With a warm smile, Nancy told Wasai to make himself at home and beckoned Janet to follow her. Trailing Nancy to the kitchen, Janet silently vowed to reach out more going forward. She tapped Nancy on the shoulder and pulled her into a hug, "I've been such a terrible friend. I'm so sorry! How have you been?"

"Not at all! You are exactly the friend I needed. I asked you for space and you gave it to me. You have no idea how much that means to me. You know my family. When John died, they descended! After a month of steady drop-ins and casseroles, I was so relieved to have the house to myself. Of course, then I really started to miss John. While everyone was buzzing around, it felt unreal. Like he was away on another fishing trip. That's why I needed to be alone. To feel him gone and start processing things. Besides, when I'm alone, I can talk to him!" Nancy laughed, "Don't worry, he doesn't answer. But I know what he'd say, so I can pretend he does. The hardest part is doing the day-to-day things alone after sharing them for 34 years."

Tears welled up in Janet's eyes as she felt Nancy's loneliness. She eased back from the hug and looked Nancy in the eye. "What about everything else? Are you still working? Are things OK…you know…financially?"

Nancy smiled. "Strangely enough, that's been the least of my worries. About 10 years ago John and I were introduced to a financial advisor. Since then, we went from over-extended credit cards, no savings and huge risk exposure to a solid footing. If we hadn't met her when we did, losing John so soon would have wiped me out financially on top of the emotional hit. She even helped with the admin stuff I just couldn't handle right after he died – she was a godsend!"

Janet was glad, but definitely surprised. "I didn't know you and John worked with a financial advisor. You never mentioned it. I've thought about it – I wish - but Wasai hates to talk about money. Maybe you could tell him what you just told me!"

With one arm around Janet's shoulder, Nancy handed her a glass of fruit punch and picked up a second one from the kitchen counter. "Here, let's take Wasai a drink and I'll tell you both all about it."

In the living room, Wasai sat in John's favourite La-Z-Boy armchair avoiding eye contact with the two women perched on the edge of the sofa beside him. Fortunately, they were deep in conversation and had given up on trying to include him. He wondered why he agreed to come with Janet today. Clearly the other husbands had stayed home. Unless, he suddenly thought, they were all widows. What if he was the only husband still living among Nancy's group friends. Was that possible? Before his anxiety could peak, Janet and Nancy appeared in front of him and Janet handed him a glass of something cold and pinkish. He took a cautious sip and then another. Seeing Nancy standing there without John by her side filled him with sadness. He didn't make friends easily and John and Nancy had been two people he felt truly comfortable with, especially John. It was still so hard to believe he was gone.

"Nancy." Wasai pushed up out of the deep armchair, placing his glass on the side table, "I don't know what to say. John was a good man." His throat felt tight as he gave Nancy a clumsy one-armed hug.

"It's okay. I can't find the words either. Never dreamed we'd lose him so soon…59 is just too young. It's good to see you sitting in his chair." Nancy smiled. "Makes me feel like he's still here with us."

Janet realized that Wasai probably didn't know how to respond to that, so she turned to Nancy. "We've been thinking about you a lot lately. Wondering how you'd manage on your own. It's so good to know that everything has been taken care of."

Nancy recognized her cue and once again shared what she'd told Janet in the kitchen. She elaborated, adding details about the wills and Powers of Attorney (POA) they'd put in place; the critical illness insurance that helped pay for cancer drugs that weren't covered; she even mentioned the savings they had put aside for their grandson's education. She then told Wasai about everything her advisor had done since John's death, from helping sort out the CPP survivor benefit to working through the banking paperwork and estate taxation. The list of supports and resources her advisor had provided or sourced was impressive.

Grateful for the change of subject, Wasai listened to Nancy, intently. He thought about John and the unexpectedness of his death. He thought about the 'maybe widows" in Nancy's living room and he thought about Janet and their children. He was almost as surprised as Janet was, when he suddenly interrupted Nancy to ask for the contact information of her financial advisor.

With an understanding smile, Nancy glanced from Wasai to Janet. "I'll just go get her card."

Key Takeaways

1. **Work with a financial advisor:** It pays to find a good financial advisor – both in terms of improved financial circumstances and in greater peace of mind. The fact is, even the most financially astute individual probably does not have the level of expertise that a professional financial advisor brings to the table. Besides, how do you find the time to focus on the complexities of building a financial roadmap when life is already so busy and demanding.

2. **Ask a friend:** One of the best ways to find a good financial advisor is by asking friends you trust and respect. If someone you trust and respect is happy with their financial advisor, they are typically delighted to provide you with contact information or an introduction. At the same time, many people will not offer that information unless asked. So, it's up to you to ask.

1. **Be referable:** Every financial advisor knows that the strongest practice is built on referrals. But referrals will only come if you are referable. That means demonstrating value and respect in all dealings with your clients: being worthy of their trust and professional in all you do. It means staying current and being the fully informed resource they count on. Above all, it means understanding your clients' needs and acting only in their best interest.

2. **Be accessible:** Of course, even if your clients consider you eminently referable, they won't refer you if they think you are too busy to take on new clients. If you are still building your practice, make sure your current clients know that you are open to taking on new clients.

3. **Honour your clients trust in you:** Remember, when clients refer a friend or family member to you, they are trusting you with that relationship—as well as testing your relationship with them!

Failing to follow up, or treating the referral with anything less than your best, dishonours both your clients and whomever they have referred to you.

Notes and Questions

Notes and Questions

3. FIRST MEETING

Sitting at the kitchen table in their modest three-bedroom bungalow, Janet and Wasai both felt a little queasy about their upcoming appointment with Sally Brandon, Financial Advisor, RFP, CLU…also known as "Nancy's god-send".

Almost as soon as he had agreed to the meeting, Wasai regretted it. He hated talking about money. It was a topic his family never discussed. Questions about anything financial were quickly shut down by his parents, who considered any such inquiries rude and intrusive. Janet's family was a lot more comfortable discussing family finances, but she'd learned early on to avoid such conversations with Wasai.

Janet wasn't nervous about meeting the advisor, she was just afraid Wasai would clam up and be difficult given the purpose of the meeting.

When Janet called to set up the appointment, Sally said their first meeting would be about getting to know each other. She would ask a lot of questions about their current situation, and try to understand what they would like to accomplish. To help them prepare and gather information in advance, Sally provided the following simple agenda for their first meeting:

First Meeting Agenda

1. Review where you are currently
2. Identify your objectives, intents and desires
3. Examine time horizons and needs for each age season (stage of life)
4. Look at cash flow as a homework piece for 2nd meeting

It was the content of this agenda, sent by email the previous week, and the accompanying list of documents Sally asked them to make available, that had both Janet and Wasai feeling uncomfortable. The agenda looked deceptively simple, but it was not going to be easy to discuss things they had always avoided talking about with a stranger. Aside from occasional oblique references to "good bill months" and "bad bill months," their finances were a mystery to Janet. Both paycheques went into one joint account by automatic deposit and Wasai took it from there. They both used a credit card for most purchases and Wasai withdrew a little cash each month for day-to-day purchases that couldn't be charged. Whenever there was paperwork to be signed, Wasai would review it, sign it and push it across the table for Janet's signature. She had learned not to ask a lot of questions about what she was signing, because he would get angry, taking offense at what he saw as a lack of trust.

Sally was due to arrive in a few minutes. Janet took a deep breath and looked at Wasai, who sat silently, staring at his hands where they lay folded on top of a yellow folder. "Are those the statements Sally asked us to have ready?"

Wasai glanced up at Janet and then dropped his gaze again. He was embarrassed. His wife would soon find out just how little he had put aside for their future. But it had been all he could do to stay on top of expenses and subsidize university fees. Whenever he started to get ahead of the bills, the car would break down or a major house repair came along. He sighed deeply and slid the folder across the table. "Here," he mumbled "I'm sorry I did not do better."

Janet opened the folder and examined the papers inside. There were statements for Registered Retirement Savings Plans (RRSP) in both their names, some Canada savings bonds and a bank savings account statement. It was not a huge amount of money, but she had always thought their only asset was real estate. She looked up and grinned, "This is a nice surprise!"

Before Wasai could respond, the doorbell rang. Feeling a little less stressed about the coming meeting, they went to answer the door.

Wasai and Janet opened the door. This financial advisor they were so anxious about stood on the front porch wearing a light spring suit the colour of new leaves and a friendly smile. She barely topped 5'4' and looked a lot like someone Janet might meet at her monthly book club meeting— except for the professional-looking tan leather satchel in her left hand. Wasai opened the door wide and gestured for Sally to come in. They shook hands, made introductions and Janet suggested they move into the living room, or perhaps the kitchen.

"Let's go with the kitchen," said Sally, with a warm smile. "It's always my favourite room."

As they settled themselves around the round kitchen table, Janet suddenly jumped back up. "Oh, where are my manners? Would you like coffee or tea? Dark roast coffee or black tea – I'm afraid we don't do decaffeinated."

"Tea would be lovely. Thank you!"

"Perfect. We're big tea drinkers, so I'll make a pot."

As Janet arranged cups, a sugar bowl and small pitcher of milk on a tray, Sally chatted with Wasai. She asked who was responsible for the front garden, already filled with crocus, tulips, and daffodils. Happy to talk about one of his passions, Wasai opened up about his ever-expanding garden, sharing his vision to eventually have perennials blooming each month, from March through November.

Surprised at how well Wasai and Sally were getting along, Janet relaxed as she filled the teapot and placed a selection of cookies on a plate. Bringing it all to the table, she passed cups around and joined the conversation.

"Now that Wasai's working part-time, he can do the gardens. Flowers in front, vegetables in back. I love it – though nothing grows for me." Janet made a face and held up her thumbs, "Two black thumbs here!"

Wasai grunted and started to say something, but stopped when Sally looked down and spoke to the floor, "Well, hello there." Vegas, their calico cat responded with a satisfied purr as he rubbed up against Sally's leg.

Wasai and Janet shared a surprised glance. The cat was notoriously shy with strangers, usually staying out of sight until they left.

"Vegas, scat!" Janet pushed the cat aside with her foot. "You'll get fur all over her."

"Don't worry. I have two cats at home. I'm used to it." Sally was unruffled, "He's gorgeous! Why did you name him Vegas?"

"Hah!" blurted Wasai.

Janet looked a little sheepish. "I always wanted a cat, but Wasai didn't. When my friend's indoor cat got out, and then had kittens, I couldn't resist bringing one home. I knew it was a gamble and Wasai might freak out, so I named him Vegas. Turns out Wasai's a sucker for small furry creatures that adore him." She smiled and put her hand on Wasai's shoulder.

Sally laughed and stroked from Vegas's head to his tail one last time and then brought her hands back to the table. As though it was the most natural thing in the world, she took a Wet-Wipe from her satchel and cleaned her hands before selecting a cookie from the plate and sipping her tea. "So," she said, "tell me how you came to ask Nancy for my number?"

Without hesitation, Janet described the pivotal visit with Nancy, their long-time friendship with both Nancy and John, the shared devastation of John's death, and the way their conversation eventually came around to the financial impact on Nancy of being widowed at 53. Wasai said little, but nodded when Janet shared the relief she felt, knowing that Nancy was well provided for. At the time, Nancy had given Sally full credit for her sound financial situation and, more importantly, her peace of mind. Hearing Nancy's story and pondered John's death made and both Janet and Wasai feel particularly mortal. Suddenly, it seemed well past the time to do something about their own circumstances.

"So, Wasai asked for your contact information and here you are."

"Thank you for that. Nancy and John have always been some of my favourite clients. I was honoured to help them put things in order and to support Nancy through John's illness and passing. She's amazing. So strong!"

Janet and Wasai nodded in unison.

"Of course, you both know that. Nancy tells me you've been friends for almost 20 years and that I should take very good care of you. Let's begin by getting to know each other."

Sally started with a quick synopsis of her background and the people who made up her financial services practice. Wasai was impressed by her credentials and the depth of expertise on her team and Janet was pleased to hear there would always be someone available, even if Sally was not. In her work in social services, everything tended to grind to a halt if the primary contact on a case file was not available. When people were left in confusion or emotional pain because someone was on vacation, Janet found it immensely frustrating.

"I will leave these with you" Sally handed a copy of the summary she had just reviewed to each of them. "Of course, everything we talk about, today and in the future, is confidential. And, if you have any questions, now or at any time, please feel free to ask."

"Nothing I can think of right now." Do you have any questions Wasai?"

"You have a strong team. But you would be our main contact, right?"

"That's an excellent question Wasai. Depending on a client's needs, I might bring in one or more specialists from my team into our meetings. For example, I would involve Hussein, our business expert, if you owned a company and needed some expertise specific to your business. In your case, I'll be your primary contact and draw on the team's knowledge as required. Of course, they'll always be there to support you if I'm ever unable to. Does that answer your question?"

"Yes. Thank you."

"Great, now it's my turn to learn all about Janet and Wasai!"

Over the next 90 minutes, they talked about everything, from the house and the neighbourhood, to their hobbies and travel preferences. It didn't feel like an appointment so much as a conversation between new friends. Sally asked if it was okay to take notes as they talked, but she did it so unobtrusively that they hardly noticed. When it came to a discussion about savings, Wasai passed Sally his yellow folder. She opened it briefly and then put it to one side "If it's okay with you, I can take these with me to make copies and bring the originals back." And the conversation continued.

By the time she left, two hours after ringing their doorbell, Sally knew more about Janet and Wasai's life than their closest friend; including:

- the cost of running their home and the details of the small mortgage they would finally burn in two years;

- their jobs and income, including Wasai's decision to transition to part-time at 63, just last year;

- Wasai's dislike of insurance because, when his mother died the insurance company refused to pay out, causing severe hardship for his father;

- Janet's desire to travel more and Wasai's preference for gardening and fishing;

- Wasai's terror of becoming incapacitated in old age and Janet's fear of being left alone with insufficient income to support herself;

- the long-awaited grandchild their son and his wife were expecting in August and how they now worried more about being able to leave a legacy; and

- the amount of time Janet spent running errands for and taking care of her aging mother who absolutely did not want to end up in a nursing home.

Sitting again at the kitchen table after Sally left, Janet felt strangely calm, yet exhausted. Wasai realized he had spoken more in two hours than he had over the past two years. In fact, they were both astonished at how much they had shared with someone they had just met.

"That wasn't too painful, was it?" Janet, put the kettle on again. "She was easy to talk to."

"Vegas liked her." Wasai stroked the cat who had curled up in his lap. "Animals know about people."

"Nancy trusts her too. I guess that's why we felt so comfortable with her." Janet paused, "Do you think we should have told her about Sara?"

"No! Sara has nothing to do with this." Wasai stood up abruptly and stalked out of the kitchen. Vegas tumbled to the floor with an offended mrooooow!

Janet watched Wasai leave with sadness in her eyes. She wished everything could be as easily fixed as Sally seemed to think. But, in her experience, some things were just too broken.

Key Takeaways

1. **Ensure a good fit:** The financial advisor you choose to work with should represent a new, long-term relationship in your life. This person may end up working with your family members and will come to know a lot about your circumstances. An advisor's credentials and education are only part of the equation. You must be comfortable with and trust your financial advisor. If you don't feel that connection, keep looking.

2. **Ask questions:** At every stage of your relationship with a financial advisor, always ask the questions that occur to you. Leaving a question unanswered will only create unnecessary stress and worry. A good advisor loves questions because they show that you are engaged and interested in learning and they help the advisor to better understand you and your concerns.

3. **Be open:** The recommendations and plan an advisor puts together for you can only be as good as the information you provide. Once you choose to trust your advisor, be open. Provide complete information on each topic of discussion. Include the factual details required as well as your feelings and preferences about things. Holding back or being less than honest with your advisor may expose you to unnecessary risk or result in a plan that is less than ideal.

1. **Earn trust:** Every interaction with your client (or prospective client) is an opportunity to build trust. Four elements are required to generate trust:

   - Intent: You must place your clients' interest first. More importantly, you must demonstrate that you have their best interest at heart. Adhere to your professional code of conduct and share it with your clients.

- Commonality: In order to trust you, your client must be able to relate to you. This means you need to share some common ground. Take the time to find out what you have in common with your clients and engage them in conversation about these interests or characteristics you share.

- Propriety: Everyone has unwritten rules and perceptions. Be vigilant. Watch for clues and indications that reveal your client's sense of propriety and respect them. One of the most obvious example is the "shoes off at the door" practice that is common in many cultures. In these homes, entering with your shoes on is a breach of propriety that might make you harder to trust.

- Capability: The final element that will make you trustworthy is your competence to do the job. Obtain industry designations. Stay current with changes and understand how those changes will impact your clients. Keep your clients apprised of anything that affects them. Be excellent.

2. **Listen, listen, listen:** There are wonderful quotes that best illustrate this point.

> "People don't care how much you know
> until they know how much you care"
>
> ~ Theodore Roosevelt.

> "people will forget what you said,
>
> people will forget what you did,
> but people will never forget
>
> how you made them feel."
>
> ~ Maya Angelou

One of the best ways to demonstrate that you care and to make people feel valued and respected is to actively and intently listen. Besides, you can't plan for anyone until you know their circumstances, challenges, aspirations, concerns and fears. And you can't discover any of that without listening.

3. **Ensure confidentiality:** As an advisor, you know that client conversations and personal information are confidential. People's privacy is a paramount concern and the details of a client's situation must be treated with great respect. Properly secure all client information, whether on a computer or in paper form. Share information only with authorized parties, as required to serve your clients. Above all, reassure your clients that you respect their privacy and will keep discussions confidential.

4. **Welcome questions:** Encourage your clients to ask questions. Never dismiss a question or treat it as trivial. Just because something seems obvious to you does not mean it will be obvious to a client. In fact, you often learn more about what's important to a client from their questions than from any other source.

Notes and Questions

Notes and Questions

4. BACK AT THE OFFICE

As she drove back to the office, Sally mentally reviewed the next steps for Mr. and Mrs. Tanwir. First she would have to transfer all the pertinent information from her notes to her needs analysis tool. That would give her a clear picture of their current situation and highlight any remaining gaps. Starting with an accurate financial baseline was essential before developing recommendations or planning the best course of action for reaching their goals and addressing their concerns.

Of course, it was always easier if she could complete the needs analysis form at the first meeting. Some new clients were perfectly comfortable with that—usually those who had worked with a financial advisor before, or had a financial background. But Janet and Wasai had seemed quite hesitant, even uncomfortable, at first, so Sally had chosen a more conversational approach, simply jotting down notes as they chatted. She was thrilled at the way they had opened up during the meeting and felt she had successfully overcome their initial wariness. If there was one thing she had learned over the years, it was the importance of establishing trust. Without it, nothing could be accomplished.

She had also learned (as strange as it may seem), that financial planning was more about relationships and emotion than it was about money. And she was no longer surprised by the many different ways people reacted to money—having it, not having it, wanting it, giving it away, hoarding it, hiding it, feeling guilty about it... Sally sensed, during their initial conversation, that Janet and Wasai also had some interesting perspectives on money and she wondered what would gradually emerge as she got to know them better.

With that thought, she parked in front of the renovated century home that housed her financial and insurance planning practice. As she gathered her satchel and jacket from the passenger seat, Simon, one of her two junior advisors, pulled in beside her.

Sally stepped out of her white Acura MDX and closed the door. "Hi Simon! I was hoping to see you here today."

Simon waved and walked toward her. "Hey Sally – me too. I have a bunch of questions about my last appointment. Some really interesting stuff. A business owner with key person and disability insurance questions. He's even thinking about a pension or profit sharing plan for his employees." Turning back briefly to click the locks on his vehicle, Simon ran a hand through his short brown hair, "Some of it's a bit over my head!"

"Great! Lots to learn. Was this someone who attended the information session last week? Are the follow-up calls going well? And how's Luisa doing?"

Simon laughed, "Yes…really well…and excellent! But I suspect my questions will be a little harder to answer. Are you in for the rest of the day?"

"Sorry about that," Sally smiled, "Didn't mean to interrogate you. Too much in my head. Yes, I'm here for the day, but I'll be busy for the next hour or so. Can we talk over lunch?"

"Sure. Works for me."

They walked past the empty reception desk, agreed to meet in the lunchroom at noon to discuss Simon's case, and then headed to their respective offices. Sally dropped her satchel on the desk and hung her jacket on a hanger behind her door. Before settling into work, she took a minute to make a quick circuit of the building and say hello to everyone on her team. They were five in total, Simon and Luisa, her junior advisors; Hussein, her small business specialist; and Shanda, her estate planning specialist—all led by Sally, with her own expertise in critical illness and long-term care planning. Once she found the right administrative person to replace Jason, she would finally have the team she wanted. Last month, Jason had shared his decision to go back to school. She hoped to bring him back into the business again someday, but for now, he wanted to complete his MBA before deciding on a career path. In the meantime, she needed someone in the role and already had 34 resumes to review before she could start interviewing!

Grabbing a coffee from the pot in the lunchroom, Sally headed back to her desk to work on the Tanwir file while it was still fresh in her head. As she scanned her notes from their meeting that morning, she realized how many were personal comments about the couple, rather than specific financial information: *Janet doesn't know much about the family finances; Wasai likes gardening; Janet wants to travel more; they both want to help their son, especially with a first grandchild on the way, etc.*

Continuing to review her notes, Sally noticed the question mark she had placed beside their son's name—trying to remember what it was meant to remind her of. There was something Janet had started to say, something about "his sis…", but then she stopped suddenly when Wasai glared at her and interrupted. Recognizing the sudden increase in tension, Sally had let it slide, adding the question mark to remind her to revisit it at some point. It was likely not the only missing piece of information—no one shared everything!

Overall, she knew that Janet and Wasai's personal preferences and perspectives would be invaluable for her planning process. In fact, she appreciated how this conversational approach gave her so much more texture and context than she could draw from just completing forms with new clients. She would have to make sure both Simon and Luisa understood the value of taking the time to understand people and what motivates them, rather than focusing solely on the financial information.

Having said that, she still needed to get the numbers down. She filled in Wasai's information first, noting that he had already started collecting CPP ($440/mth), even though he was still working part-time and bringing in approximately $32,000. According to Janet, it wasn't his age that made him change from full to part time. Rather, he wanted to be available to help look after their first grandchild. Since Wasai hadn't identified any other sources of income, Sally moved on to fill in Janet's income information. Her $78,000 salary was their primary income right now and, at 55, she was a long way from retirement. Unlike Wasai, she didn't plan on stopping or cutting back on work any time soon.

Once the total family income was established, Sally filled in everything she had jotted down about their expenses. She made a note to ask them about certain expenses that seemed unusually high. Specifically, their utilities and property taxes seemed a little out of line, given the size and location of their home. When she added up their after-tax income and deducted the expenses, they showed monthly surplus income of about $1,800. Sally knew there was a good chance they had missed a few things, so she rounded that number down to $1,500. Right now, this monthly surplus was accumulating in their chequing account, tempting them toward impulse purchases they didn't need. Janet had described one typical example: a water filtration system they purchased from a door-to-door vendor two months earlier. Apparently, they had been talked into replacing an existing system, installed only a few years ago. Sally smiled as she recalled Janet's sheepish explanation of their tendency to make unnecessary upgrades just because they had the money available and the people at the door were so convincing. Sally was looking forward to helping them put that surplus to much better use.

The final piece of the financial puzzle was the net worth statement. Tallying up their assets and liabilities from her notes and the statements Wasai had provided, Sally calculated that the Tanwirs had a net worth of $1.2 Million, most of which was the equity in their home. What she didn't have was any information about existing insurance policies, except for those documented in their employment benefits books. She was also missing any information about their estate plans and specific retirement goals and wishes. She would email them a list of homework before their next meeting to fill in those gaps. As always, her mind immediately jumped ahead to possible strategies for improving their situation and addressing some of the concerns they had shared with her. She mentally shook herself. "Slow down Sally!" she spoke out loud, "you don't have the full picture yet."

"Uh…are you talking to me?" Luisa stood at Sally's door with her hand raised to knock, looking confused.

"No, no…just talking to myself again. What's up?"

"We just got a call from Lydia Wong, her husband has cancer. A brain tumour apparently. She said you put some kind of health insurance in place the last time you were there, but she can't remember the details. She seems pretty flustered. I told her you'd call right back."

"Oh no…Jeremy! Yes, we set up critical illness insurance. He's an IT consultant, works from home, no benefits. Lydia's off work on maternity leave with their second child – beautiful little girl – not at all shy."

"I didn't realize they're young. Cancer? That's strange!"

"I wish it were true Luisa—it's more common than you think." Sally sighed, "Let me pull their file and organize my thoughts and I'll give her a call."

Sally closed the Tanwir file, pushed it aside and turned to unlock the fireproof filing cabinet that held her active client files. She remembered the details of the critical illness policy she secured for Jeremy last year, but it was best to check before calling. The last thing Lydia needed right now was inaccurate information! Spreading the file out on her desk, she glanced at the clock as she picked up the phone. Only 15 minutes to provide a devastated young wife and mother what little consolation she could, before her lunchroom conversation with Simon. Taking a deep breath, she punched in the Wong's home number.

The conversation with Lydia was draining, but at least she'd been able to allay her financial fears. Lydia was holding up as well as could be expected under the circumstances. Still, she sounded scared, with tears hovering constantly. Sally quickly reassured her that the $200,000 critical illness policy would kick in, giving Jeremy access to every available treatment. With the right treatment, the doctors were cautiously optimistic about his prognosis. Of course, even the best-case scenario would likely mean surgery, followed by chemotherapy and, possibly, radiation. So, there would be months when Jeremy was unable to work. Lydia was afraid she would have to go back to work early. But if she did, the daycare costs for an infant and a toddler would wipe too much of her income for them to manage. Besides, then she wouldn't be there to support Jeremy.

Fortunately, one of the first insurance products Sally had recommended, when they met five years ago, was private disability and loss of income insurance for Jeremy—a standard requirement for any self-employed person and business owner. With a non-taxable income payout of 60% of his average income, and the critical illness policy covering any additional medical and caregiver expenses for Jeremy, Sally was happy to let Lydia know she could focus on taking care of her family.

Leaving Lydia in a much better frame of mind, Sally gently replaced the telephone receiver and closed her eyes. It was already 12:02, but Simon would have to cut her some slack. She needed a minute or two to recharge and wait for the wetness in her own eyes to dissipate.

Moments later, leaving the Wong's file on top of her desk to remind her to initiate the critical illness claim, she headed for the lunchroom to help Simon with his new case. Simon was already at the small round table making the most of a sandwich and a bottle of chocolate milk.

"Hi Sally, Luisa told me you got a claim call. Something about a young couple with cancer. That's rough. Are you okay?"

"Thanks Simon, I'm fine. These calls are a lot harder when I have to deliver bad news. Lydia and Jeremy are great people and they understand the point of insurance. She reads every piece of information I give her and he's determined to protect his family. Having to face cancer is terrible, but Jeremy is young and strong and they'll have the resources they need to fight back."

"Right! Good to know. So, are you okay to talk about my business owner now, or would you rather reschedule?"

"Now is fine." Sally reached into the refrigerator and pulled out an apple and a single-serve Greek yogurt. Grabbing a spoon from the drawer, she joined Simon at the table. "So, fill me in."

Simon launched into a recap of his meeting with Peter Reynolds, a local business owner with a 20-year track record and 35 employees. Although Mr. Reynolds had a piecemeal collection of insurance and investments, he had never worked with a financial advisor before. Lately he'd been attending some information seminars, like the one Simon and Louisa hosted last week on succession planning, and had conclude he needed to be more strategic about both his personal and business finances.

The discussion with Simon continued until 1:30 pm, when the alarm went off on Sally's phone. "We'll have to pick this up later, Simon. Check my online calendar and add a meeting wherever you see an hour or so open over the next few days. In the meantime, I need you to brush up on disability insurance and key person insurance, as well as individual and private pension plans and deferred profit sharing plans (DPSP). Ask Hussein where to start, he knows this stuff inside out."

"Is that all!" Simon laughed, "I'll book it for later in the week to give me enough time to study. My next meeting with Mr. Reynolds is not until the 15th."

"Okay, I'll let Hussein know you're looking for resources"

"Great - thanks!"

Sally headed back to her office, grateful that she had remembered to set the alarm on her phone when she added the meeting with Simon to her calendar. Otherwise, their conversation would have continued indefinitely. And she still had a lot to do before her 5:30 appointment this evening! First on her list was initiating the claim for Lydia and Jeremy Wong, then she had to email a list of homework to Wasai and Janet Tanwir. Hopefully she would have time to review at least some of those 34 resumes, before breaking off to prepare for her final appointment—helping a family plan for the long-term care and support of a severely autistic child.

Thinking about this next appointment and her earlier conversation with Lydia Wong, Sally once again realized how much she loved being able to help people deal with the unexpected calamities of life; the "what ifs" that settled randomly on the unsuspecting and the well-prepared alike. She had no magic formula for avoiding life's left curves, but she could definitely help people mitigate the damage by avoiding the financial catastrophe that often accompanied those arbitrary curves.

Key Takeaways

1. **Value the team:** This chapter provides a window into the way a team-based financial services practice works. The combination of skills, perspectives and expertise offered by such a practice adds great value for clients. While it can be gratifying to have the undivided attention of one personal financial advisor, having a whole team on your side means better access, enhanced customer service, continuity of relationships, and deeper expertise.

1. **Never assume**: Inaccurate assumptions about what is normal or common in a particular demographic can be costly to your clients. It's important to base your recommendations on facts and evidence, not your instinctive understanding of a situation. Once you do understand the facts, make sure to fully inform clients of the benefits and risks of purchasing a particular product—and the benefits and risks of not purchasing it. Make sure your client has all the information needed to make an informed decision.

2. **Offer Options:** There is seldom one perfect solution to any financial challenge. Do your homework and distill the information available into a few good options. Describe the advantages and disadvantages of each option and help your client determine the best possible fit given their circumstances, preferences and risk tolerance.

3. **No one knows everything:** Financial services is a vast and complex field. Expecting to know everything about every aspect of your clients' financial needs is unrealistic. Collaborate. Draw on the expertise of your team, if you have one. If you don't, cultivate a pool of experts who you can call on or refer to when you need information that is outside your area of expertise.

Notes and Questions

Notes and Questions

5. HOMEWORK

Both Janet and Wasai knew they were fortunate. A single day at work was enough to reinforce that fact for both of them. Not that they didn't face challenges. No one was that blessed! But they had a comfortable home, food on the table and a steady income. Many of the people who came through the Hopewell Centre, where Janet managed a team of family and youth counsellors, were not so lucky. Wasai also saw the effects of poverty and society's shortcomings daily, while driving his bus through the downtown core.

Their relative prosperity made Janet feel a bit guilty for stressing about anything financial. But it was important to stay on top of these things. She knew, better than most, the distance between stability and financial disaster was not far. Every day she saw people's lives thrown into turmoil. All it took was the loss of a job, a protracted illness, an expensive habit or someone making a single bad decision. It was time she and Wasai took charge of their own circumstances rather than relying on continued good fortune.

As for Wasai, he just knew he never wanted to live like the people he saw struggling—so close to the bone. He could not forget his own years of poverty, nagged by the constant, gnawing hunger of an underfed pre-adolescent. His parents had sacrificed everything to keep him in school and eventually send him abroad to study. Although he didn't become a rich doctor, as they hoped, he did build a good life for himself and his family. Once settled, he had tried to help his parents immigrate too; but when it came to making the decision, they said they were too old to leave the world they knew and start over in a strange place. Even bringing them over for a visit, when Ali was born, had not been enough to convince them to come. Wasai had continued to coax, especially when his mother's heart gave out and his father was left alone. In the end, his parents were born, lived and died within a radius of fifty miles—aside from those three visits to their "prosperous son with the white wife" in Canada.

All this reminiscing and soul searching was new territory for Wasai and Janet. In fact, most of their conversations (both internal and external!) had been different since meeting with Sally. For one thing, they were talking more about money than they ever had. And both were thinking more about the financial implications of retirement, grandparenthood and aging in general. Now that Janet knew about the savings Wasai had put away over the years, she wanted to know what it would mean for their retirement and whether she needed to keep working for another ten years. She also told him about the automatic savings plan she had been contributing to at work. Apparently, they had both been doing their part to provide for the future, despite their silence on the subject. Of course, Janet didn't mention how she dipped into that workplace savings account to send a birthday gift to Sara each year, and to buy a present for the wedding Wasai still refused to accept. She wondered if she would ever be able to share that secret with him, or with Ali for that matter.

On this particular Saturday morning, Janet and Wasai sat on the back patio, enjoying an unusually warm spring morning and a cup of tea. The idyllic morning heightened their sense of well-being and encouraged a reflective state of mind. The financial threads, weaving in and out of every thought, were undoubtedly triggered by the list of homework Sally emailed the day before. The list, which Janet had printed late last night, sat on the round, glass-topped table between them, waiting to be addressed.

Homework for Wasai and Janet

During our next meeting, we will review the following:

- Any insurance policies you have in place. We'll look at everything to make sure you have the right coverage at the right price.
- Wills, and Powers of Attorney for both financial and personal care. We will discuss your estate planning priorities and make sure they are captured.
- Copies of property tax and utility bills (I have a couple of questions about these).
- Any other financial documents we may have missed in our first meeting.

I'd also like you to think about your retirement goals, so we can chat about:

- When you would like to retire (or fully retire for you Wasai!).
- What you hope retirement will look like.
- Where you want to be and/or go when you retire.
- Family involvement and/or obligations that may play a part in your retirement.

Finally, can you please pull together any information you have about your work pension or group RRSP. If you do have a pension plan, we will need whatever information you can get for calculating how much you will receive when you fully retire.

As usual, Janet was the first to say something. "Do we have everything she's asking for? You still have that one life insurance policy from when Ali was born, don't you? And there's the car and house policies. I know we did our wills when my father died, 11...no...12 years ago. Oh! Do we still have Nancy and John listed as guardians for the children?"

Noticing Wasai's continued silence, Janet stopped and looked at him, waiting.

"Which question do you want me to answer?" Wasai crossed his arms across his chest with a stubborn frown.

"All of them!" Janet reached over and nudged his shoulder. "Come on grouchy, I know you hate this stuff, but we need to get serious. We're not getting any younger…especially you!" Janet sprang up from her chair with a playful smile. "I'll put the kettle on, you find the paperwork…more tea or do you want coffee this time?"

"Hmph, coffee." Wasai pushed his chair back. "Really strong coffee!"

As she headed to the kitchen, Janet sighed. This was going to be tough. Even though he had agreed to work with Sally, Wasai was still resisting. She could only imagine the emotional can of worms they would open by looking at the will! Janet found herself wishing, as she had so many times before, that both her husband and son would be less rigid and more compassionate. In fact, Ali was the real stumbling block. She often wondered how her open-hearted, loving son had become so intolerant. She knew Wasai was a marshmallow at heart and would relent if Ali would stop reinforcing his rejection of Sara and her life choices. In the meantime, all Janet could do was hope and pray that all this recent reflection would soften Wasai's heart and help him accept what he could not change.

Janet cleared her mind and headed back outside. She called to Wasai to open the screen door, as she balanced a tray with another pot of tea, a French press full of dark roast coffee, two cups and a small plate of Wasai's favourite Peek Freans, Fruit Creme biscuits.

Wasai's eyes lit up when he saw the biscuits. Taking the tray from Janet's hands, he placed it on the table, sliding aside a fat yellow folder. "Cookies and coffee first. Annoying paperwork later!"

For the next half hour or so, Janet and Wasai enjoyed the quiet of their yard and the warm spring sunshine. They watched a pair of industrious robins fly back and forth, collecting bits of grass and twigs for the nest they were clearly building in the maple tree at the back of the yard. An occasional sparrow stopped to drink from the small concrete bird bath Wasai installed last summer. Fingers touching, they shared a deep appreciation for the peace of the moment. Until, in the distance, someone started up a gas lawnmower for the first cut of the season and the tranquil spell was broken.

Draining the last of his coffee, Wasai cleared the table, placing the tray of empty dishes on a small table, off to one side. He drew the fat yellow folder toward him. "Okay, let's look."

They had one life insurance policy on Wasai. The document in the folder said "5 Year Term Insurance" with a "death benefit" of $250,000. According to Wasai, the premium for this policy was currently $234 per month, but it increased every five years and would go up again in two years, when he turned 65. It would also lapse at age70. Just thinking about the money he'd put into it over the years made him angry. It also reminded him of his father's financial struggles, when his mother died and the insurance company refused to pay out on the small policy purchased to cover funeral costs. Wasai would have cancelled his policy years ago, but ever since the doctor put him on Coumadin to prevent blood clots, Janet was worried about his health and how she would manage if anything happened to him. It didn't help that a friend told her Wasai was now uninsurable because of his condition.

Although the yellow folder was thick with 25 years of annual statements from the insurance company, there was no life insurance policy for Janet. Back when Janet and the insurance agent had convinced Wasai to buy the policy to protect his family, Janet was a stay-at-home mom. Wasai felt it didn't make sense to insure someone who was making no income and nothing Janet or the agent could say would convince him otherwise. Besides, he was hostile toward insurance in general and agreeing to the policy on his own life was the most he would concede. The insurance agent didn't push it. In fact, they hadn't heard from him since.

Aside from the one term policy, the only other insurance on themselves was the $25,000 of automatic life insurance that came with their respective employment benefits. Of course, that would end when they retired.

Next, Wasai pulled out the home and auto insurance policy. Fortunately, they were both good drivers with no recent claims and, since Janet turned 55, they both got the experienced driver discount. By keeping their two cars and two properties with one insurer, they benefitted from an additional discount. Wasai was pretty sure he had done a good job with this bit of their finances.

The last item in the file was a manila envelope from the lawyer who had drawn up their wills 12 years ago. Wills had never crossed their minds until

Janet's father died unexpectedly, from complications after hip surgery. Janet's mom, Elizabeth, had been devastated and overwhelmed, even though her husband had left things in good order. Watching her struggle and knowing how much worse it could have been made Wasai receptive when Janet said they should do their wills. Especially with the children to think about. Apparently, it took the death of someone close to make them pay attention to these things!

Wasai pulled the will and POA forms from the envelope. He read through them, silently passing each one to Janet as he finished. They were pretty standard. In the will, they named each other as executors, identifying John and Nancy as alternates. Janet had forgotten about that. At the time, neither of them had family nearby and Nancy was Janet's best friend. The will itself was simple. They left everything to each other, and to their "existing and future children" in trust if they both died. Nancy and John were also named as guardians and trustees for the children. The situation was similar for the Powers of Attorney, except the alternate identified as substitute decision maker was Janet's sister, who had since moved to Belize. So much had changed!

Janet dropped the last of the papers on the table. She knew they had to talk about this. Wasai would likely want Ali to be their alternate executor now. They definitely didn't need the guardians or the trust for minors, unless they wanted to put in something for "existing and future grandchildren." And clearly her sister couldn't be their alternate for the POAs anymore. It would be way too inconvenient for her. Janet was also considering giving something to the two charities she volunteered with. And then, of course, there was the problem of Sara. Two questions repeated over and over in her mind…

How were they going to get through this?

Did Sally have any idea what she was getting into?

But these were questions for another day. Right now, she had to clear away the evidence of their morning activities, tidy the house and prepare the backyard for guests. This afternoon they were hosting the family to celebrate her mother's birthday. Nothing fancy, just a late lunch in the yard, a few gifts and Elizabeth's favourite dessert, strawberry shortcake, made with the first fat, organic berries of the season.

"We'll have to come back to this Wasai. Mom will be here in two hours." Janet tidied the papers back into the folder, tucking it under her arm. She lifted the tray of dishes from the side table. "Can you grab the door for me?"

Wasai walked slowly over to the patio door and opened the screen. Stepping out of Janet's way, he seemed lost in thought as he watched two sparrows dipping thirsty beaks into the water in the bird bath. Janet put everything on the kitchen counter, shook her head and walked back to close the screen door. "Wasai, you're letting the flies in!"

Wasai did not respond, staring silently at the birdbath even though the birds had flown away to other spring pursuits. No doubt, they were off to find food for hungry chicks. Helpless, squalling, chicks who demand so much until they learn to fly and leave the nest. He wondered if the sparrows felt abandoned once the nest was empty.

Reading the will this morning, thinking about the plans they had made to protect their children, watching robins build a nest and sparrows refresh themselves before foraging—everything today made him think about Sara. His beautiful baby girl. From the moment she was born, his heart was lost.

He was so proud of Ali, his focused, serious firstborn son; yet Sara, the mischievous imp, with her huge, coffee-brown eyes and long dark hair that curled into soft ringlets, was the light of his life. While he demanded much of Ali, who worked hard to earn his respect and attention, Sara could do no wrong, and he could never stay angry with her. No matter what she got into, he would instantly forgive her when she climbed into his lap and wrapped her little arms around his neck. Everyone, even Ali, was easily won over by Sara's charm. She may have been a little willful, but she was also warm, loving and generous—never hurtful. At least, not until that day, four years ago, in her final year of University, when she dropped a bombshell onto their family dinner table. His beautiful little girl told them she was gay and would like to introduce them to her life partner.

That night was the first time he lost his temper with her, lashing out in his confusion and pain, and the last time she had been home. So secure in their love, Sara had shared her news with confidence and then left in devastation, with only her mother's stunned but sympathetic embrace to soften the pain. Caught in the cold vacuum of her absence, Wasai missed her with every breath, but the words he flogged her with that night could not be taken back. Yet he could not accept the finality of her announcement. He hoped desperately that separation from her family would bring her to her senses. That one day she would come home, wrap her arms around his neck once again and tell him it was just a phase she had to go through.

Four years and her wedding had gone by since that night and still they hadn't talked. It didn't help that Ali adamantly opposed any involvement with Sara as long as she was with "that woman." At first, Wasai thought Ali was just being supportive, but it soon became clear that Ali was even more horrified by Sara's homosexuality than Wasai was. As for Janet, he did not know how she felt about the situation, since he cut her off every time she tried to raise the subject. He realized avoidance would not work much longer. Talking about retirement, grandchildren and especially wills, would soon force the issue. And he'd rather figure out their answers before Sally started asking the questions. He wondered, once again, how a stranger could make them talk about things they had never discussed and make them excavate their most painful secrets. He hated it, but had a feeling it was necessary medicine.

Janet's voice roused him from his musings. "Wasai, could you give me a hand please? Mom just called, she's coming early and we need to wrap these gifts!" Grateful for the distraction, Wasai blinked the moisture from his eyes and joined her in the kitchen.

Key takeaways

1. **Examine your relationship with money:** Think about what money means to you and how you use it.

    a. Do you think of it as a source of security or freedom?

    b. Are you more inclined to spend money today and let tomorrow look after itself, or the opposite—saving all your money for tomorrow while denying yourself any financial flexibility today?

    c. Do you watch your pennies closely, or are you inclined to waste money?

    d. Most importantly, does money mean the same thing to you and the others in your life, or does it become a source of conflict in your relationships.

    Before you can commit to a successful financial plan, it helps to understand the role money plays in your life.

2. **Be prepared:** An advisor can only plan well if she has all the necessary information about your situation. Even if it makes you feel like a student being asked to complete an unpleasant assignment, take the time to pull together the information your advisor asks for. Much like a doctor diagnosing an illness, for a financial advisor, understanding the whole picture improves accuracy and ensures the most effective response. You can support the process by being prepared and bringing all the relevant information to the appointment.

3. **Know what matters:** Throughout the financial planning process, you must make decisions—not all of them financial! You may have to choose between an ideal future, and a future you can afford. You may have to choose between indulgences today and security tomorrow. You may have to choose between helping others and helping yourself. These are not easy decisions and you will have to think seriously about what really matters to you. Sometimes, these decisions are not yours alone, so you may need

to negotiate or compromise if your priorities are not in line with the priorities of others, who are also impacted by these decisions.

FOR ADVISORS

1. **Be holistic:** Approach each client with a spirit of discovery. Set out to understand the whole picture before jumping to solutions. To use the doctor analogy once again, treating symptoms without understanding the underlying illness may make the patient feel better temporarily, but it doesn't make him well. It's important not to let your own desire for a "quick fix" get in the way of understanding the broader situation. As Stephen Covey says, "Seek first to understand." Once you understand, you can create a plan to address the source of the symptoms instead of just offering a short-term band-aid solution.

2. **Offer clear guidance:** Remember that your clients come to you for a reason. If they knew what to do and how to accomplish their financial goals alone, they would not reach out to a professional for help.

    a. Make sure they understand the purpose behind your questions and information gathering.

    b. Provide resources to illustrate concepts and take the time to explain clearly.

    Your purpose is not to dazzle them with your brilliance, but, rather, to shine a light on and simplify complexity, so they can move forward.

3. **Encourage the exploration:** Sometimes a financial advisor is tempted to rush the process, especially with clients who are very trusting. But taking shortcuts early in the relationship will often lead to discord later. You may also leave significant issues hidden. If your clients don't ask themselves the important questions, ask for them. If your clients don't question what you tell them, confirm understanding before moving on. Make it safe for your clients to join you on a personal voyage of discovery.

Notes and Questions

_____

_____

_____

_____

_____

_____

_____

_____

_____

Notes and Questions

6. FAMILY GATHERING

Always early, Ali and his very pregnant wife, Fariah, arrived first. Janet helped her daughter-in-law get comfortable, commiserating with her about swollen ankles and sleepless nights. While they caught up, Ali helped his dad take extra chairs out to the patio, since it would be a shame to waste such a glorious spring day by staying cooped up inside. They had just added the finishing touches—three colourful Happy Birthday balloons tied to the rose trellis—when Janet noticed a taxi pulling up in front of the house. She was surprised to see her mother exit the cab, clutching a small bouquet of flowers in one hand and her purse in the other. Just turning 76, her mother still looked lovely. As usual, she was dressed immaculately: today it was a lightweight lilac suit with navy trim that matched both her handbag and shoes. Yes, Elizabeth Starkey knew how to make a good impression. Stopping for a moment on the front walk; she straightened her jacket, patted her hair into place and turned toward the house.

As Janet stepped out onto the front porch, she noticed how white her mom's hair had become. There was no trace of the rich chestnut brown waves that used to cascade over her shoulders. At least the short, practical cut accentuated the curl, softening and flattering her mother's strong features. Janet also noticed her mom's slight hesitation at the bottom of the porch steps; the way she moved her purse up onto her forearm and shifted the flowers, leaving one hand free to hold the handrail before stepping up. These signs of frailty disturbed Janet, especially since her mom lived alone

49

in the house where Janet grew up. It was too big and too much work, but her mom refused to leave it.

"Happy Birthday Mom!" Janet opened her arms and drew her mother into a warm hug.

Handing the flowers to her daughter, Elizabeth stopped on the porch to catch her breath. "Seems those stairs get steeper every time I visit. You'll want to put those in water so they don't wilt – the cab was too hot for them."

"Thanks mom. You know you don't need to bring flowers every time you visit. Especially on your birthday! It's our day to give you gifts."

"I'm too old for birthdays. I'm only here because you bribed me with strawberry shortcake." Elizabeth smiled when she saw Fariah, standing inside the screen door. "And to see my beautiful grand-daughter-in-law, who's going to make me a great-grandmother very soon."

Fariah grinned back at her. "Hello Elizabeth. Happy Birthday!" She held the door open as Janet and Elizabeth entered. "You'll be the most beautiful and stylish great-grandmother ever."

"Hah! Flattery will get you everywhere! Don't worry, I'll spoil that baby regardless. No need to butter me up."

The three women moved to the kitchen where Janet found a vase for the flowers. As she arranged the combination of lilies, carnations and baby's breath, she gently probed to find out how her mom was doing. Although they spoke on the phone every few days, Janet soon realized her mom kept a lot to herself. Not only was her arthritis acting up, making it difficult to walk up and down stairs, the doctor had also cautioned her about the potential for falls. So, with the help of a long-time neighbour, she had moved her bedroom to the main floor and no longer ventured upstairs. Unfortunately, the laundry room was still in the basement, leaving Elizabeth dependent on that same helpful neighbour to come and run a load or two on the weekends. Of course, she still insisted on washing her undergarments by hand in the bathroom sink and hanging them to dry on the towel rack. She wasn't quite ready to have someone else handle those.

"Mom!" Janet wailed, "How could I not know about this? Why didn't you tell me?"

"You have enough to do without running over to my place to move furniture or do laundry on your day off. Besides, it never occurred to me to tell you."

"Well make sure it occurs to you next time!"

"I've been taking care of myself for a long time, young lady! I'm still your mother and I don't need your permission or your blessing."

Mother and daughter glared at each other in silence until Fariah broke in with a chuckle: "Wow, you two are so much alike! Ali is proud and stubborn too—now I know where he gets it."

For a moment, it looked like Elizabeth would take offense at Fariah's comments, but her expression relaxed and she made a sound that would have been a snort coming from anyone less elegant. "You are growing my great-grandbaby, so I will let that pass. Janet, let's not talk about this anymore. It's spoiling my birthday"

Janet was about to let it go, when she suddenly remembered the taxi. "Mom, why did you come by cab today? Where's your car?"

Elizabeth shrank visibly, like a balloon with a slow leak. "I had an accident. I don't want to talk about it."

Janet couldn't bear to see her indomitable mother looking so cowed, but before she could respond, Wasai and Ali came in from the backyard and the moment passed.

"Here's the birthday girl! Happy Birthday Grandma!" Ali wrapped his grandmother in a hug, while Wasai added a more subdued birthday greeting.

They soon moved out to the patio, where the conversation shifted to best birthday stories and future birthday plans for the family's pending addition. Elizabeth opened her gifts, most of which consisted of gift cards for the local bookstore and her favourite gourmet food bistro. Until one box remained. This was clearly not a gift card. Elizabeth carefully removed the ornate wrapping paper, pulling tape off slowly to preserve it. Everyone fidgeted as she smoothed and folded the paper and put it to one side. Opening the cardboard box, Elizabeth picked up the envelope that lay on top of the Styrofoam packing material. When she opened the envelope to read the card inside, tears sprang to her eyes. "It's from Sara."

Ignoring the sudden silence, Elizabeth lifted out the beautiful inlaid, walnut writing box that was nestled in the Styrofoam bed. "This is absolutely perfect! Janet…Wasai…your daughter is the most generous, thoughtful and sensitive person I know. You really must get over this ridiculous bias of yours and welcome her back. I miss her dreadfully. And so do you…No. Ali, don't say a word! You'll spoil my birthday."

Everyone stayed silent. Elizabeth continued her delighted examination of the writing box, seemingly oblivious to the tension around her. Wasai glanced anxiously at Ali, who sprang up from the table and strode angrily to the back of the yard. Janet and Fariah exchanged a worried look and then began clearing away the dishes, still sticky with traces of whipped cream and blood-red strawberry juice.

Sad to see the day slide into discord and angst, Janet beckoned her mother back into the kitchen. "Bring the writing box with you, I'd like to take a closer look as soon as I wash the sticky off my hands."

Together, the three woman explored the nooks and crannies of the gorgeous box; exclaiming over the heavy, cream-coloured stationery and delicate note cards Sara had thoughtfully added.

Elizabeth beamed with pleasure over the gift. "I've always wanted a writing box like this. I'll write Sara a thank you note as soon as I get home."

Janet looked at her mother and murmured, "Please give her my love."

Pretending not to hear, Fariah stared through the screen door at her proud and stubborn husband, who was still glaring at the tulips and daffodils in the back garden. Then she turned to watch her father-in-law for a moment. He sat, slumped at the patio table, looking a little lost and forlorn. She noted the compassion in Elizabeth's eyes as she promised to write to her daughter's daughter, passing on a secret message of love. Finally, she looked down at her swollen belly and wondered how the complications of family would affect her baby.

Shaking off the emotions of the day, Janet offered to drive her mother home to save the cost of another cab ride. She called the men in from the yard and they overcame their own feelings long enough to wish Elizabeth a final, if somewhat subdued, Happy Birthday. Placing the birthday cards and gift cards inside the writing box, Janet tucked the box under one arm and gently grasped her mothers arm to help her down the front porch stairs before helping her into the passenger seat of her Blue Corolla. Waving to the solemn group on the porch, they drove off.

As they pulled out of the driveway, Janet glanced over at her mother. "What happened with the car?"

Elizabeth looked down at her hands, clenched in her lap and sighed deeply. "I don't know, exactly." She sighed again, still looking down. "I pulled out of the driveway, checked my mirrors—all of them—checked again—then backed into a parked car that wasn't there! It just didn't show up in the mirrors."

"Did you check over your shoulder too?"

"No." Elizabeth looked at Janet sheepishly, "The arthritis, in my neck is getting worse. It hurts to look over my shoulder."

"Oh mom. Are you okay? Were you hurt? Was there a lot of damage?"

"I'm fine. It was a very slow crash. Barely scratched my bumper, but crumpled the side panel of the neighbour's Honda. My fault, so my insurance premium will skyrocket. I'll have to give up the car. Between this and the doctor, I guess it's time.'

"The doctor? What did the doctor say?"

"Well, my dear, it seems I have a side of glaucoma to go with the many other indignities of aging. A few weeks ago, I asked the doctor to test my balance because I kept tripping over Misty. Apparently, my balance is okay, but I'm losing peripheral vision. The dog was literally blindsiding me. The doctor suggested I stop driving—and now, with this accident, he'll make it official."

"I'm so sorry mom. Why didn't you tell me you were dealing with all of this?"

"You have enough on your plate. Besides, what could you do? Stop me getting old? Anyway, I don't want to talk about it anymore. I'm ancient history. You have the future to deal with."

For a while, neither of them spoke and then Elizabeth took a deep breath and broke the silence. "Janet, when are you going to tell them."

"I don't know mom. Wasai doesn't even know I keep in touch with

Sara. I think I have to ease into it."

"You know how excited he is about grandchildren. It's one of the main reasons he's so upset about Sara's life choices. He says it goes against his religion, but so does having a mortgage, marrying you, drinking beer…and he's done all that! No. He doesn't want Sara to be gay because he imagined her married to a nice young man, surrounded by his grandbabies. Maybe the picture will never include the 'nice young man' but he needs to know it will soon include at least one more grandchild!"

Janet remained silent, wondering why life had to be so complicated. Between her mom's gradual decline, the advent of a new generation and her family's generally confused feelings about Sara, some days Janet just wanted to be alone—to experience a single, uninterrupted moment of complete peace. But that wouldn't be today. Or tomorrow for that matter. Tomorrow they would meet with Sally again. And before then, before they started discussing wills, insurance (and now) aging parents, with their financial advisor, Janet would have to tell her husband that both Ali and Sara would soon be parents.

Key Takeaways

1. **Accept that families are complicated:** While still the primary social unit in most societies around the world, there is no such thing as a simple family. This is not a recent phenomenon. Families have always been complicated. Every tradition has its stories of family solidarity, sacrifice and betrayal. And today is no different. Just consider this small selection of quotes about family:

> *"There's nothing that makes you more insane than family. Or more happy. Or more exasperated. Or more... secure."*
>
> *~ Jim Butcher*

> *"Begin with your own family"*
>
> *~ Sayings of Spartan women*

> *"Your children are not your children. They are the sons and daughters of Life's longing for itself. They came through you but not from you and though they are with you yet they belong not to you."*
>
> *~ Kahil Gibran*

> *"A little more than kin, and less than kind"*
>
> *~ Shakespeare*

> *"Siblings: children of the same parents, each of whom is perfectly normal until they get together."*
>
> *~ Sam Levenson*

"It takes a whole village to raise a child"

~ African proverb

"I've remembered that most of life is about small, essential connections, so unobtrusive, so elastic, that you scarcely realize they're actually holding you together. The big ones-the great, grand emotional bonds-those are the ones that break, the ones that fail you, the ones that give way and send you careening toward the foot of the bleak and jagged canyon. It's the tough, gnarled, unadorned ties that really do bind, that never let you fall all the way down into darkness."

~ Sharon Shinn

Whatever the composition of your family, it will likely have an impact on your financial planning process and the decisions you choose to make. Whether you are raising young children, taking care of elderly parents, or trying to understand the life choices of your adult children; if you have a family, those relationships, however tenuous, will influence you. That influence may be minor or shattering; unsettling or enlightening. Either way, be prepared to be surprised and stretched by the power of family when you decide to put your financial house in order.

FOR ADVISORS

1. **Accept that families are complicated:** A financial advisor and the exploratory financial planning process often serve as catalysts within a family: creating the spark that triggers dialogue on topics previously avoided or disregarded. Unless you are working with an individual who has no family ties at all, you will need to understand the main elements of your client's family situation to be effective. As you explore those dynamics, remember to tread lightly when your clients bring both new and long-buried reactions into the conversation. When you come to the table as a financial advisor, never underestimate the impact of family on the planning process and on the final decisions your client will make.

Notes and Questions

Notes and Questions

7. SECOND MEETING

At 8:00 am, Monday morning, Sally's team gathered in the lunchroom. Rather than crowding into her office for their weekly team meetings, Sally preferred to have everyone gather around the circular lunchroom table, with fresh coffee and bagels close at hand. It made the obligatory staff meetings more collegial. S&H Financial was her company and she was ultimately responsible for the ethical behaviour and regulatory compliance of everyone on her team, but she had never been comfortable with top-down management. Besides, she had always found collaboration and mutual accountability more effective than command and control.

That being said, as usual, the first item on the agenda at this Monday's meeting was compliance. Always a highly regulated industry, Financial Services had been through a major upheaval since the global financial meltdown in 2008. It was Sally's responsibility to make sure everyone on her team was aware of industry trends and regulatory changes. Topics on her radar this week included the implications of financial technology (FinTech) for both clients and advisors, the "Best Interest Standard" discussion paper recently published by the Canadian Securities Administrators, and global trends affecting International Capital Standards.

She would also touch on recent policy and procedural changes at certain insurance and fund companies they worked with. Finally, Monday meetings were also when she addressed any concerns about the quality of paperwork, client files, customer service, etc. Sally knew she had a great team, because these issues were rare and easily overcome with additional training and coaching.

The compliance review went smoothly, with only a few questions about how global risk management changes would affect Canadian companies and whether that would impact their clients[3]. After fielding those questions, Sally pushed the thick compliance folder to one side. "Okay, now that we've covered compliance and administration—everyone grab a coffee top-up and we can get to the good stuff."

Sally smiled as she watched everyone come back to the table with renewed energy, eager for the best part of their Monday morning staff meetings. They spent the next 90 minutes sharing cases, brainstorming ideas, discussing new products and strategies, and identifying ways to improve on every aspect of the business. Sally knew this was the true value of these weekly meetings. Each member of the team brought different life experience and industry expertise to the table. Their combined knowledge was the greatest asset of the practice and, more importantly, of their clients. Licensing, initial training, one-on-one coaching and ongoing education were all essential to the development of competent, professional advisors, but these group brainstorming and problem-solving sessions were true gold.

Cognizant of the time, Sally interjected, "Great discussion everyone! Just a few final items before we wrap up. Luisa, I love your idea about partnering with a law firm for our next business succession planning seminar. Hussein, Shanda, can you please help Luisa organize that by reaching out to your networks for someone with the best fit? Simon, check your calendar and let me know if you're available to sit in on some interviews on Wednesday and Thursday this week. We really need to replace Jason! I've short-listed six candidates and would like two team members to help me pick a winner. Shanda and I have already cleared our calendars for those two days. I hope you can make it work."

---

[3] Minimal at this point. More information available at
http://www.canadianunderwriter.ca/insurance/osfi-staff-actively-engaged-international-capital-standard-insurers-zelmer-1004089347/

Simon immediately pulled out his mobile and checked his schedule for the week. "I'm good. Just a couple of things I can move around…Okay, I've blocked off both days for interviews…But you'll be asking the questions, right?"

"Don't worry Simon. I just want you to observe and give me your opinion afterwards."

Simon relaxed visibly and grinned. "That, I can do!"

"Great. Thanks Simon. One last thing before we get back to work. I'd like to share something I read last week. You all know Harley Lockhart, past chair of Advocis and a financial advisor for…well…forever! I came across a profile on him in Forum magazine. Something the author wrote about his approach struck a chord with me and I think it's something we should all embrace. I'll read it to you.

> *'Putting clients' interests first has always been a given for Lockhart, whose website states that the focus of his practice is "… to enhance my clients' quality of life by reducing financial stress." Lockhart provides insurance solutions to clients and works with them to understand the sources of their financial stress, which he has found is often the result of a disconnect between their values and where they spend their money. "Many people don't recognize what's important to them," he explains. "It's about [helping them to] prioritize."'*[4]

That's exactly what we do. We help people. We're stress-busters! Now go—do some good this week!"

Laughing, the team scattered. Sally could hear Simon and Luisa chanting "Who you gonna call? Stress busters!" as they boogied down the hall and back to their desks.

Gathering her files, Sally rinsed her coffee cup and filled it with water before returning to her office. She had one hour before her coaching session with Luisa. That should be enough time to prepare some good questions for the interview candidates. Then, if she reviewed the Tanwir file over lunch, she could still touch base with Hussein and Simon before leaving for her 2:00 PM meeting with Wasai and Janet. Sally wanted to make sure Simon was fully prepared for the meeting with Jim Reynolds on Tuesday morning and this would be her last chance to talk to him today.

---

[4] Forum Magazine, March 2013 issue, Profile: Straight Up by Kristin Doucet

She was pleased that Simon asked Hussein to join him for that meeting. Simon would take the lead, since Mr., Reynolds was his client, but bringing the team's business specialist along as a resource was ideal. With Hussein's expertise and Simon's analytical intelligence, Mr. Reynolds and his business would be in good hands.

When Luisa showed up at her office door at 11:00 am sharp, Sally was just finishing up the interview questions and a list of skills she felt would be critical for a successful office administrator. Although everyone on the team was pitching in since Jason left, they were all feeling the lack of administrative support. The sooner she could bring someone on board, the better. Sally glanced up from her computer screen, "Hi, Luisa – I'll be right with you."

Luisa pulled up a chair. "No worries."

Closing and saving the file, Sally turned from her computer to give Luisa her full attention. "So, how is everything going? Last week you were a little overwhelmed with the seminar follow up."

"It's better, much better. Simon and I spent some time planning our approach like you suggested. That helped a lot. You were right, when we stuck with the priorities of the people we called, we were much more effective. That's why we convinced Hussein and Shanda to tweak the seminar response cards: right after the feedback section, we added a list of key areas of interest that people can check off when they ask for follow up. Now we can really zoom in on what matters to them when we call. It's made a huge difference in the quality of the calls and the number of appointments."

"Excellent! That's what I like to hear. Remember to keep that client focus at the center of everything you do and it will all come together."

"Thanks Sally. What you're saying makes so much sense to me, but every time I come back from a conference, I feel like I'm missing the boat. So many of the other agents and advisors are focused on the numbers and pushing the 'latest and greatest' product."

"Luisa, you're not missing the boat, they are. If you prioritize the product instead of the person, you may make the sale, but you'll lose the relationship. We're in it for the long haul not the quick sale."

Luisa nodded. "That's what I like about working here. That and the fact we outnumber the guys! So many men in dark suits at those conferences!"

"Even that's changing Luisa. The Insured Retirement Institute did a study in 2013 that showed 70% of women seeking a financial advisor prefer to deal with a woman. Since women are expected to control two thirds of the wealth in the U.S. by 2020[5] and the Canadian market is similar, we'll be in high demand! Besides, women make excellent financial advisors and the role offers the kind of flexibility and autonomy many women want. I truly believe we're in the right place at the right time."

"Awesome! Just don't tell Simon and Hussein they're heading for obsolescence; I like working with them and still have lots to learn."

"Hah! No need to worry about that. I'm keeping all of you." As if on cue, Sally's phone alarm pinged. "Time to get back to work. What's on your plate this afternoon?"

"I just got a call from a friend who had a baby last month. Suddenly, she wants to talk about insurance." Luisa grinned as she stood up to leave. "Apparently, the biological clock and the financial planning clock are connected."

"Remember, take time to understand her situation. Don't jump to a solution, even if it seems obvious."

"Yes Ma'am!" Luisa sketched a mock salute and walked briskly out the door.

Sally watched the youngest member of her team stride down the hall and poke her head in at Simon's door. She was pleased with Luisa's progress. The young woman absorbed information like a sponge, accepted both direction and advice eagerly and was committed to making a difference for her clients. And Sally loved the way she brought a new, fresh perspective to the team. It wasn't easy to get Hussein and Shanda to try new ideas—with over ten years in the business, they tended toward an "if it ain't broke, don't fix it" mindset—yet somehow Luisa managed to bring them around. That ability was worth cultivating. Like so many of her business clients, Sally wondered who would take over her practice when she retired. Perhaps Luisa could be part of her own succession planning, she

---

[5] Source: US Federal Reserve

mused, filing the thought for later.

Shifting gears once again, Sally went to grab her habitual yogurt and apple from the lunchroom refrigerator. She brought them back to her office and opened the Tanwir file to refresh her memory for her two o'clock appointment. Mainly, she wanted to make sure she had a clear list of additional questions and discussion points to cover. She reviewed the budget and balance sheet she had prepared, using a lime green highlighter to mark the items she wanted to talk about. On her copy of the homework list, she circled wills, property tax, utilities and retirement income to remind herself to delve into those areas. Closing the file, she slipped it into her satchel along with her notebook computer. Sally then took fifteen quiet minutes to finish her lunch, listen to some music and breathe.

With her satchel in hand, Sally headed for Simon's office, stopping briefly to ask Hussein to join them. Simon sat with the file open on his desk. As Sally and Hussein entered, Simon swivelled his computer monitor so they could see the projections he had prepared. Simon and Hussein walked Sally through the options they had out together for Mr. Reynolds.

They had proposed a revised insurance portfolio that provided protection for both his family and his business in the event of his death, injury or illness. Although this involved replacing existing life insurance policies and adding disability and critical illness coverage, Simon was able to demonstrate that the total cost of ownership of the enhanced portfolio would actually be less than his current coverage, over the anticipated life of the policies.

Since the business was overly dependent on Mr. Reynold's knowledge and expertise, Hussein had outlined a succession planning process that would help him put the right people in place to step up and carry on the business in the event of an emergency, or should he decide to retire.

Finally, they had included an analysis describing the relative merits and limitations of a private pension, a deferred profit sharing plan and a group RRSP as potential retirement savings benefits, to round out the company's existing employee benefits package.

Sally was pleased. "Excellent work! Simon, how did you find the process? Any challenges?"

"The pension and DPSP stuff was a bit daunting." Simon grinned, "So much government gobbledygook. But I just peppered Hussein with questions, right Hussein?"

With a deadpan stare that belied the smile in his eyes, Hussein muttered, "Gobbledygook…is that a technical term?"

Sally laughed. "I can see you two are getting along famously. This looks great. Good luck tomorrow! I'm gone now for the rest of the afternoon, but I'll check email before the end of the day if you have any questions." Satchel in hand, Sally waved to Simon and Hussein and headed for her car.

With the mild spring weather, the summer construction season had already started and she was forced to detour twice on her way to the Tanwir's place. Fortunately, she always built in a time buffer and pulled into their driveway at 1:55pm. Turning her mobile to silent, Sally did a quick check in the mirror, tossed her keys into the satchel and got out of the car. Smoothing the travel wrinkles from her skirt, she adjusted her jacket and headed up the front walk. As she stepped up onto the front porch, the inside door opened and Janet smiled a tentative welcome through the screen. Sally could see Wasai hovering in the hallway behind Janet's shoulder.

Sally reached for the screen door as Janet opened it. "Hello Janet. Hello Wasai. How are you this glorious spring afternoon? Wasai, your garden looks incredible! And the lilac buds already smell delicious." Sally stepped into the front foyer.

Janet smiled. "Wasai planted them for me when we bought the house. Lilacs are my favourite. They don't last long though, so I'll be putting them in vases all through the house as soon as they open."

"Absolutely delightful! Wasai, you are a gardening wizard."

Wasai looked pleased and a little embarrassed. "Please come in," he gestured toward the kitchen. "We were just making tea."

They sat around the kitchen table, as they had on Sally's first visit. Wasai chose the same chair with one hand resting on a yellow file folder, just like the one he'd given Sally before. Janet placed the teapot, three cups, two plates of cookies, the sugar bowl and small creamer jug on the table, just as she had the last time. Sally found the sensation of déjà vu almost overwhelming. When the cat, Vegas, slid in from the other room and started winding around her ankles, she truly felt she'd gone back in time. She shook herself back into the present and wondered why both Janet and Wasai seemed to have retreated behind a wall of formality once again.

"So, Wasai, I see you have some more paperwork for me. Before we get into it, I'd like to review the budget[6] I put together from our last meeting, to make sure everything was captured accurately. Is that okay?"

Wasai's shoulders lost some of their tension. "Certainly, let's do that."

"Here, I made copies so we can all look at it together. Give it a quick review and let me know if anything jumps out at you that needs to be corrected. Then I have a couple of questions."

In a few moments Janet and Wasai looked up from papers in front of them. They exchanged a few words and then turned to Sally.

Janet spoke first. "It looks pretty complete to me. It's strange, I don't remember talking about the details last time, but I guess we must have. Seeing the numbers in black and white like this makes me realize how much money we must be wasting each month."

"What about you Wasai? Do the numbers look right to you?"

Wasai turned to Sally. "Yes, I think so. Maybe we spend a little more than $150 on restaurant meals each month. We like to take Ali and Fariah to dinner sometimes. To make sure they are eating well. I think we should double that."

Sally made a note on her copy of the budget. "I do have a couple of questions. First, what information were you able to gather about your work pensions?" She took the pension plan booklets and two separate sheets of paper from Wasai and quickly reviewed the retirement income estimates they showed. "Excellent! You'll both have pension income too." She placed the papers on the table in front of her.

"My next question is about current expenses. Both the property tax and utility numbers you shared with me seem high for this house. Did you pull together copies of the tax and utility bills?"

---

[6] Background information, detailed budgets, net worth statements, retirement income projections and insurance needs worksheets for Wasai and Janet Tanwir are available at www.whathappensifbook.com.

Janet looked at Wasai, seeming a little perplexed. Wasai opened the yellow file folder and passed a pile of tax and utility statements over to Sally. As Sally began flipping through them, Janet suddenly sat up. "Of course, we forgot to tell you about the rental property! Wasai bought a small house for Ali and a couple of his schoolmates to stay in while attending university. We planned to sell it when he graduated, but Nancy and John suggested it made more sense to keep it as an investment. Wasai, you must have lumped them together."

Sally turned to Wasai. "Is that the case?"

Wasai nodded, "Yes, that's right. 35% of the property tax and utility numbers in the budget are for that rental property. The rest is this house."

"Ah, that makes sense. So how much is the rental income from this property, and are there any other expenses we've missed?"

"So far there have been no big expenses. The house is rented to a young family. They take very good care of it. They pay $1,500 rent, utilities included, and they cover their own cable and internet costs."

"Is there a mortgage on the property?"

"No, we paid cash. Janet's father listed her as beneficiary on one insurance policy and her mother on another. It was just enough to pay for a small townhouse when Ali went off to school, so we didn't have to take on more debt."

Sally jotted down the additional information. "So this means you have additional cash flow of over $1,000 per month that we haven't captured in this budget. Are you claiming this rental income on your taxes?"

Wasai's back stiffened, "Of course we are!"

"You'd be surprised how many people don't know they have to claim rental income. I'm glad you're on top of it. No one needs unpleasant surprises from the CRA! Could you share your tax returns for the last couple of years with me so I can make sure we capture this additional information?"

"I will go get them." Wasai stood up and left the room abruptly.

Janet looked at Sally. "He's a little sensitive about taxes. When he became a landed immigrant in Canada, he didn't know he was supposed to file tax returns every year. He ended up filing three years at once; paying the back taxes, interest and penalties. It took him two years working an extra job to pay it off."

"Hmm, sorry I touched a sensitive spot."

"It's not your fault." Janet sighed, "He's feeling pretty sensitive about everything today."

Before Sally could ask Janet to elaborate, Wasai returned, dropping three large white envelopes on the table in front of her. "Here are our tax returns for the past three years."

"Thank you! You obviously have a good handle on these things."

Slightly mollified, Wasai sat down and reached for a biscuit. Sipping his tea, he glanced over at Sally and muttered, "Sorry, taxes make me edgy."

Sally laughed. "Me too, Wasai, me too."

Adding the tax returns to her growing pile of paper, Sally jotted down a few more notes and then put her pen down. "Okay, let's look at the insurance policies."

Wasai opened the yellow folder and pulled out two envelopes, which he passed to Sally. One envelope contained the details of their home and auto insurance. Sally was pleased to see that the policies were comprehensive and included replacement cost coverage, sufficient liability limits and extra accident benefits on the auto policy. She checked that the rental property was also insured. The policy premiums were reasonable for the coverage. Wasai had clearly done his homework when it came to their general insurance needs.

But Sally couldn't say the same for their personal insurance coverage: with only one substantive policy on Wasai, they were not well protected. And Term 5 was one of the most expensive term insurance options available. Sally didn't even count their work coverage. At $25,000 it was nominal and would expire as soon as they retired if they didn't convert to private coverage. In their circumstances, Sally would also have liked to see some critical illness coverage—and a reasonable amount of life insurance—on Janet since she was currently the main income earner. Sally looked up from her notes. "May I borrow the life insurance policy as a reference? Your home and auto policies are in great shape, but I'd like a copy of this policy on hand when I look into insurance planning options for you."

Wasai nodded. "You can keep it. I'm thinking of cancelling it anyway!"

"Why would you do that?"

"Life insurance is a scam. You pay into it for years and then they refuse to pay your family when you die."

"Ah. I see. You've clearly had a bad experience. Would you be comfortable sharing what happened?"

Wasai told the story of his father's frustration with the insurance company that didn't pay when his mother died and the financial hardship it caused his father.

"What a terrible situation! I'm so sorry your family had to deal with that on top of your loss. It's true, some insurers are not reliable. Especially in countries where the industry is not well regulated. I'm sure you know that Canada has one of the strongest, most well-regulated financial industries in the world. Even so, it's important to deal with stable companies who have a track record of honouring their policies." She held up his life insurance policy. "This company is strong and reputable."

Wasai shrugged, "I know. It just makes me so angry when I think about it."

"I'm not surprised. I would be furious in that situation."

Having been quiet for some time, Janet reached for Wasai's hand "You were right to get this policy. When Ali was a baby and I wasn't working. You wanted to protect your family—just like your father did."

The three of them sat in silence for a moment, as if paying their respects to the memory of Wasai's parents. Then Janet jumped up. "I'll put the kettle on and make a new pot of tea."

Wasai, stood up. "I need a bathroom break. I will be right back."

As soon as Wasai left the room, Janet turned to Sally and started talking rapidly. "I need to tell you something before he comes back and we look at the wills. We have a daughter, Sara. She's 24 and lives in Winnipeg. Four years ago, she 'came out' over dinner. Wasai and Ali went a little crazy and haven't spoken to her since." Janet continued breathlessly with one eye on the door. "Two years ago she married her life partner, and now they're going to have a baby—I'm not sure how that works, but Sara is pregnant. I just told Wasai about the baby yesterday. He's stunned and really conflicted. Ali doesn't know yet, but I don't think he'll react well." Janet heard the bathroom door open and stopped talking.

Sally whispered, "Wow! I thought you might have another child and wondered why she was never mentioned. Thanks for the heads up."

Janet's shoulder-length hair fell forward, hiding her flushed cheeks as she reached to refill the tea cups. Wasai came back into the kitchen. Apparently unaware of the heightened tension in the room, he sat down and reached for another biscuit. "Okay, what's next?"

Sally caught Janet's eye and gave her a reassuring nod. "Before we look at your wills, I'd like to spend some time exploring your vision for retirement and beyond. In your homework, I asked you to consider when you plan to fully retire and how you see yourselves spending your retirement years. I'd also like to understand what your hopes are for leaving a legacy."

For the next while they talked through various scenarios. Sally took notes and interjected with questions occasionally to keep the conversation flowing. A few clear desires emerged from their discussion:

1. Wasai would likely fully retire in two years if not sooner, while Janet planned to work for at least another five years, and as many as ten if necessary.

2. When they retired, they envisioned a quiet life of reading, gardening and playing with grandchildren, with a couple of short trips (1-2 weeks) each year for Janet's benefit.

3. They wanted to stay in their home as long as possible, especially while they were both alive, but they never wanted to become a burden.

4. They both felt it would make sense to sell the rental property when Janet retired, since neither of them wanted the ongoing responsibility of being a landlord as they aged.

5. It was more important to them to help family and leave a legacy than to live in luxury.

6. Janet was worried about her mother's declining health and how that might impact her over the next few years, especially if her mom needed more care and support while Janet was still working.

After confirming that she had accurately captured their wishes, Sally took a deep breath. "Okay, so let's look at your wills and Powers of Attorney."

Wasai slid the folder over to Sally. The legal-sized envelope was the only remaining item in it. Sally slid the pile of paper out of the envelope and pored over the wills. Wasai concentrated on the cup in front of him and Janet held his hand under the table.

"These are pretty straight forward, although clearly out of date with the trust and guardianship provision for minor children." Sally placed the documents on the table and folded her hands on top of them. She spoke gently, looking directly at Wasai. "You had two children when these wills were written. You've told me so much about Ali, but haven't mentioned your daughter. Can you tell me what happened?"

Janet looked at her husband with tears welling in her eyes. "It's okay. She'll understand. You know we have to figure this out."

Wasai stared at the table. Finally, he wrapped both hands around his teacup as if warding off a chill. He took a deep breath and stared into the cup as if the tea would offer answers. "I don't know what happened. She was my little girl. Beautiful, smart, happy. She went off to university and changed into something I don't understand. One day she came home and told us she was homosexual, a lesbian. That she loved a woman. I couldn't make the idea fit into my head. It felt all wrong. I said terrible things to her—called my little girl an abomination. I told her she was an insult to her family and that she should leave. So, she left."

Wasai glanced up, then quickly hung his head again so Sally wouldn't see the tears he was holding back. "Ali was even worse. He used vicious, foul words I never thought to hear from his mouth. We haven't seen or spoken to Sara since that night." He glared briefly at Janet "But apparently, Janet has. Now she tells me Sara and that woman are going to have a baby. How is that even possible? Another grandchild. My Sara's baby. No father, two mothers. I don't know what to think." Wasai pushed the teacup aside and dropped his head into his hands.

Sally gave him a moment to compose himself. "The world can be a confusing and complicated place sometimes Wasai. What a challenge for your family! Although, I confess, I was afraid you would tell me your daughter had died in a car accident or from some horrible disease. At least Sara is alive. And soon she'll have a child, your grandchild."

Sally turned to Janet. "I know this is hard for both of you and I don't need to know this minute, but you must decide whether taking care of family and leaving a legacy also applies to Sara and any children she may have. You'll have to talk about it and let me know before I come back, so I know what to build into your plan."

"Yes, I know. But how do we include Sara? Ali will be the executor of our wills. As the eldest adult son, he'd be offended if we chose anyone else. And he'll be furious if we leave anything to Sara. In his mind, she's not family anymore!"

Wasai looked up wearily, "Maybe the baby will change him. Only a parent can know what it feels like to have your heart ripped out by your child—yet still want to hold her in your arms."

Janet walked around behind Wasai and wrapped her arms around his shoulders. He sagged back against her. Sally fought her own emotions as they comforted each other. After a minute of charged silence, she decided to wrap things up and give them space. "Janet…Wasai…there is so much love in your family; I'm hopeful this rift will eventually be healed. Until then, there are things we can do to allow you to include Sara and her child in your plans, without offending Ali. I'll provide some suggestions when we come back together. For now, I think we should call it a day."

Janet turned to Sally with a sad smile, "I bet you didn't see this coming."

Sally slowly slid the pile of paperwork from the table into her satchel and stood up. "Every family has its challenges. And every client has a story. It's part of what makes my work so interesting and satisfying. If I can help you and Wasai overcome these obstacles as you plan for your future and your family, I will have done my job. It's what gives me purpose."

"Thank you Sally. This has been tough, but necessary. And we appreciate your understanding."

Wasai nodded, but remained silent as he pushed his chair out and stood up. The three of them walked to the front door and said their subdued goodbyes. As Sally backed out of the driveway she could see Janet and Wasai still standing at the front door, leaning into each other like two trees firmly rooted, yet each dependent on the other for support.

Key Takeaways

1. **Know yourself:** Whether planning for retirement, deciding what kind of legacy (if any) you want to leave behind or building a protective fence around your family, it's essential to know yourself and what matters most to you. For example, if you're a person who must be busy and socially active to feel fulfilled, you need to build that into your post retirement lifestyle. Expecting to be a different person just because you are no longer working is unrealistic and can lead to a frustrating and disheartening retirement experience. The same applies to estate planning. Take the time think about your relationship with family and community. Consider whether you are more motivated by living life to the fullest, leaving a substantive legacy or creating a balance between the two. As you design your financial roadmap, be sure the route and destination you choose truly reflects where you want to go and how you want to get there.

2. **Accept support:** In this life, no journey is made in complete solitude and no goal is accomplished entirely alone. There is no disgrace in asking for help and accepting support when it is offered. In fact, by allowing others to help you, you also give them permission to seek your help when they need a hand. Author T.A. Webb says it best: "A burden shared is a burden halved."

3. **Do the work:** When you decide to put your financial house in order, "the work" will likely include digging through files, organizing paperwork, reviewing numbers, talking to lawyers, thinking about taxes, taking a close look at (and maybe changing) spending habits, etc. More importantly, it will require thinking about and discussing important life issues with those who are closest to you—ideally, leaving no dark corner unexplored. Finally, if your efforts are to set you on a better road, doing the work means making decisions and taking action.

1. **Keep learning:** Good financial advisors are lifelong learners. Aside from the fact that both financial products and the industry itself are constantly changing, so is life and the world we live in. Cultivate and feed a hunger for knowledge. No two lives are the same, no two families are the same, and no two client situations are the same. If you approach your practice and the people you serve with an open, enquiring mind, every moment will be a learning moment, even when you're the expert at the table.

2. **Expect emotion:** You might think discussing finances is pretty dry stuff. But when it comes to money and its ability to effect lives, people will get emotional. When you are invited into someone's home to help them plan their financial future, most of the topics you delve into will be fraught with emotion. You will talk about family, life, money, debt, taxes, health, aging and death. You will learn more about your clients than their best friends. How could it not involve emotion?

3. **Be (or become) sensitive:** Because the topics you discuss with clients are private, personal and emotionally-laden, sensitivity and emotional intelligence are critical assets for a financial advisor. If your default reaction to a display of emotion is an overwhelming desire to say "snap out of it!" you'd be well advised to cultivate these essential skills.

Notes and Questions

Notes and Questions

Notes and Questions

8. THE ROADMAP

Sally had planned to go back to the office and start working on the Tanwir's plan right away, but after their emotionally draining afternoon, she decided to make it an early night. As she pondered the never-ending complications of family dynamics, the lure of a long, mindless soak in a fragrant tub soon became overwhelming. She would just have to make up for it by going in extra early in the morning.

Back at the house, Janet and Wasai stood together in the doorway for a while after watching Sally drive away, and then slowly made their way back to the kitchen. While Janet cleared away the dishes and wiped the table, Wasai tidied up the few remaining documents. They both worked silently, until Wasai turned to leave the room and Janet finally spoke. "You know she can't fix this, right? She can help with the financial stuff, but she can't put our family back together. That's up to us."

Wasai stared at the floor for a moment and then looked up at Janet with sad, bewildered eyes. "I know, but how?"

Drying her hands on a dishtowel, Janet came over to Wasai and wrapped him in a hug. "Don't worry, we'll figure it out. In the meantime, let's focus on what we can do." She hesitated, "How about giving Sara a call to see how she's doing?"

Wasai immediately stiffened in Janet's arms.

"If you're not ready to talk to her yet, I'll put her on speaker. You can just listen. Wouldn't it be good to hear her voice?"

Wasai's spine relaxed slightly and he nodded. "Okay. But you can't tell her I'm listening."

Janet smiled into her husband's shoulder and thought—we'll get there, one step at a time—even if they're baby steps.

*****

On Tuesday morning, Sally arrived at the office before 7:00 am with her satchel slung over her shoulder and her hands wrapped around a large Chai latte. Early mornings, when the office was empty, were her most productive time. And her decision to relax and recharge the night before was clearly a good one. She felt like she could take on the world today. Even the Tanwir's complicated family situation didn't seem as daunting as it had the night before. The shared office calendar showed everyone else out at appointments all morning, so the office was hers for at least five hours. Perfect!

Unloading everything on to her desk, she sat down to organize her thoughts. When putting together a plan for any client, Sally followed a standard five step process.

1. Gain a clear picture of the current situation (including budget and cash flow, debt, savings and assets, net worth and the personal realities and dynamics at play).

2. Determine financial goals and desires and related timelines (including major purchases, anticipated expenses, as well as lifestyle, health and wellness, retirement and legacy goals.)

3. Identify gaps between the current and desired situations

4. Create a plan that addresses the identified gaps and builds on the

four compass points of financial security:

    a. risk management

    b. emergency/opportunity funds

    c. long-term and retirement assets

    d. estate planning.

5. Implement the plan and monitor the client's evolving situation— modifying the plan as required to stay on track.

Sally was confident she had a good sense of the Tanwir's current situation, both financially and personally, as well as their various life goals. Of course, there were some unusual family dynamics to take into account, but that was not uncommon. First, she would have to update the budget and net worth statements to account for the rental property and a few minor expense changes. Then she'd run the numbers on their anticipated retirement income to determine any shortfall. She knew those numbers would look much better with either the rental income or an injection of capital from selling the rental property. And the combined company pensions would make that forecast even stronger. She was always amazed at the impact of a company pension. After updating the numbers, she could tackle the more complex challenge of providing for the unexpected and getting past the current discord. Waiting for her computer to boot, Sally sipped her frothy Chai and leaned back in her chair, letting things roll around in her mind.

Sally spent the next hour or so entering information and checking the numbers. Once everything was considered, she was pleased to see that the Tanwirs could count on meeting their post retirement needs, even if Janet decided to retire in five years instead of ten. Of course, working the extra five years would make their retirement much more comfortable and enable them to better protect themselves and provide for their family.

Based on Sally's calculations, the proceeds from the sale of the rental property could generate enough additional retirement income to meet their needs without eroding the principal. This offered several benefits:

- an emergency fund;
- the ability to transfer allowable amounts into the tax free savings

account (TFSA) each year and enhance the non-taxable portion of their investment income;

- the option to increase the income stream as they get older, when preserving capital becomes less critical;

- the opportunity to preserve the value of their estate for their heirs.

These were all possibilities they could discuss over time. The first leg of their financial road map would focus on putting their immediate concerns to rest and their surplus income (before and after retirement), to better use.

Sally continued to compile her notes, building on the four-point framework she preferred. In the area of risk management, she proposed the following recommendations:

1. Purchase permanent life insurance for both Wasai and Janet. Since their pensions would provide a 66% survivor benefit after the death of either annuitant, this insurance would help make up the difference in lost pension income for the surviving spouse. The most cost effective approach for achieving this would be a joint, first-to-die permanent policy that would provide a small top-up when the survivor benefit reduction kicked in. Purchase critical illness insurance for both Wasai and Janet to protect against the costs associated with catastrophic illness.

2. Discuss their preferences regarding long-term care should it become necessary. Depending on the level and cost of care they desire, determine whether long-term care insurance is advisable. Since both Janet and Wasai had expressed some concerns about being a burden as they age, Sally decided she would include a quote for their consideration.

For building emergency/opportunity funds Sally had three key recommendations:

1. Set up a separate savings account and transfer all surplus income out of the current account (aside from a reasonable cushion to avoid overdraft). Ideally, "out of sight" would mean "out of mind," helping them to avoid unnecessary impulsive purchases.

2. Set up TFSA for both Janet and Wasai and use the proceeds from

the sale of the rental property when Janet retires to top them up. These funds would accumulate tax free and provide tax free retirement income. They will also serve as a fund for emergencies and big purchases in the future (e.g. new car, home repairs, etc.). In advance of Janet's retirement, they should start the migration to tax-free savings by shifting their Canada Savings Bonds and savings accounts to TFSAs. In prior years, Wasai split the interest income on the bonds between the two of them for tax purposes. Although the tax on this income was minimal, it was tax they didn't have to pay.

3. Once the grandchildren are born, establish Registered Education Savings Plans (RESP) for them. This would be a concrete way to directly benefit the grandchildren.

Happily, retirement income (one of their main concerns), was not going to be a problem. With their pensions, anticipated CPP and OAS benefits and projected investment income, their retirement income needs would be adequately met, although the projections were a little tight if Janet decided to retire early. Regarding retirement savings, Sally had only one recommendation, and it would probably surprise the Tanwirs. Although they had little annual contribution room due to large pension adjustments, Wasai had done his best to put something into RRSPs each year. And now, Sally would recommend that he discontinue that practice.

1. Stop contributing to RRSPs and redirect those funds to one or more of their other objectives (appropriate insurance premiums, TFSAs, RESPs, more travel, or building tax sheltered cash value within a permanent insurance product). Because they will both have sufficient retirement income, any money they take from an RRSP later will be taxed at their full marginal tax rate. Building additional retirement assets that will not be taxed (TFSA), or enhancing insurance protection is the better strategy in this circumstance.

Finally, with respect to estate planning, Sally jotted down a number of recommendations:

1. Update the wills to reflect their current reality: change of executor, distribution of assets, removal of guardians for minors, addition of desired charitable donations, etc.

2. Update Powers of Attorney, appointing new substitute decision makers for both financial and personal care.

3. After assessing the tax impact on the final disposition of their combined estate, Sally determined that the impact would be limited to probate fees, taxation of any remaining RRSPs and any unrealized gains on their remaining investments (if applicable). Since they would be drawing down the value both their registered and non-registered investments during retirement, Sally projected a tax and fee liability of less than $100,000 in the estate. She would share this information and let them decide whether they want to put additional insurance in place to cover those taxes and fees or accept that their heirs would inherit the after-tax value of the estate.

4. Put a reasonable estate equalization insurance policy in place to provide a legacy to Sara and her child outside of the estate; thus, preventing conflict with Ali. (Note: confirm that this would be an interim strategy based on Ali being the executor and still feeling hostile toward his sister. Ideally, over time, the rift can be healed and the estate distribution normalized with an updated will).

Satisfied that she had a strong initial roadmap for the Tanwirs, Sally shut down her computer and put the file away. As she locked the filing cabinet drawer, she heard voices in the reception area. She quickly recognized the voices of Luisa and Simon, caught up in their usual bantering. Closing her office door behind her, Sally joined them as they moved toward the lunchroom. 'Hi guys! How was your morning?"

"Great!"

"Awesome! Hearing about trends effecting our industry was fascinating. Technology, taxes, regulations – everything's changing!"

"Exactly. That's why you had to be there. You two started your careers in very interesting times. I'm eager to hear your thoughts and ideas about what you learned."

"We're about to grab lunch. Join us? We can give you a run down."

"Thanks Luisa, I'll be right there." As Sally entered the ladies room she called back over her shoulder, "Remind me to tell you about our new admin person!"

Back in the lunchroom, they discussed the implications of current and imminent industry trends, while they ate. As digital natives, Luisa and Simon were excited about the many self-service options being generated by new technologies. Sally understood the attraction of speed and convenience, but worried about the loss of relationship and wondered how clients like Janet and Tanwir would fare with a technology driven process. She suspected that a combination of personal touch and innovative technologies was likely the best for her clients. Of course, the biggest challenge was maintaining the right balance for her clients and her business in the face of this tsunami of change.

"Sounds like a good session. And you asked some great questions. Before the next staff meeting, think about how we might respond to what's happening. How we can best serve our clients in this changing environment? I'm attending the same presentation with Hussein and Shanda tomorrow night. So, next Monday, we'll put our heads together and strategize."

"Sounds good." Luisa and Simon stood up to leave.

"Wait—you forgot to remind me! Our new admin person. Her name is Lai Yee Cheng and she starts on Monday. I'm so excited! She was the best of five strong candidates. Simon, you saw the interview. Three relevant co-op placements: TD Bank, Manulife and a small insurance brokerage. She likes administration. She's keen to get licensed and sees this as a long-term career opportunity. What's not to love?"

"That's great news! She was my top pick too – smart, confident and very personable."

"Hooray, someone to help with the paperwork!" Luisa did a happy dance and wrapped Sally in a hug "Couldn't be happier boss!"

Watching them head down the hall, Sally laughed and thought about the new addition to her team. She would spend some time over the weekend preparing to onboard Lai Yee. First impressions on a new job were a two-way street. She wanted to make sure Lai Yee's first few days were interesting, challenging and overwhelmingly positive. It had been hard managing after Jason left and Sally was looking forward to having a good right arm again! In the meantime, she had three new appointments to prepare for and conduct, payroll to run and the report for the Tanwirs to compose, all before Thursday.

*****

When Sally pulled into the Tanwirs' driveway, the first thing she noticed was the riot of lilacs that had fully bloomed since the week before. Three lush bushes enfolded the front porch in blossoms ranging from white to deep purple. As she stepped out of her car, the fragrance wrapped around her and she stopped to breathe it in. Seeing her standing motionless at the bottom of the front porch steps, Vegas seized the opportunity to rub shamelessly against her ankles. Circling, purring and alternating sides for full effect.

"Vegas! Stop that!" Sally looked up to see Wasai holding the screen door open. "Come here, you rude animal!"

"It's okay Wasai. I hardly noticed. Your lilacs are making me drunk!"

Shaking off the spell of sun-warmed spring lilacs, Sally stepped up onto the porch and greeted Wasai with a smile. "Every time I come here, there's more evidence of your amazing gardening skills. I love this smell!"

"Hah! Lilacs don't take much skill. And these are taking over the porch. Please, come in. Janet's in the kitchen."

Vegas, adept at avoiding Wasai's pseudo-wrath, darted past Sally and vanished into some secret place in the living room. As they moved into the kitchen, Janet greeted Sally with a smile and placed the tea and cookies on the table. It was beginning to feel like a welcome tradition, this tea and cookies with the Tanwirs, and Sally realized she was growing quite fond of this lovely couple.

Settling in at the kitchen table, Janet seemed in a hurry to pour the tea and pass around the cookies. As soon as everyone was settled, she spoke.

"Before we get into our stuff, could you take a look at this for me." Janet reached for a document sitting on the counter behind her and slid it across the table. "I was clearing out the second floor for my mother on Saturday. She wants to rent a bedroom for a little extra income, since she can't get upstairs anymore. I don't like the idea, but she's a stubborn woman! Anyway, I found this at the bottom of a box of old bills and bank statements. It looks like some kind of insurance, but my Dad died years ago. Do you think it's still good?"

Sally took the papers from her and looked through them. "This is excellent Janet! It's a paid-up, long-term care policy that will provide $2,000 of tax-free monthly income to your mother when she needs more support. You mentioned that she can't go upstairs anymore. Is there anything else that she can no longer do for herself?"

Janet looked confused. "What does that mean, paid-up? I don't think my mom's paid any insurance premiums since my dad died."

"The policy was purchased with a 15-year payment plan. No premiums have been required for the past five years. It's not the most common way of buying this kind of insurance, in fact, they don't offer 15 year paid up anymore, just 20. Either way, it means your mother didn't have to worry about keeping up premium payments after that 15 year period was up."

"So this policy is still good? Does that mean she can get that extra income now?"

"It depends on how she's managing her daily activities and how much help she needs. That's the way these policies work."

"Well she'll never go to a nursing home, if that's what you mean. She plans to die in that house if it kills her!"

"No. She can live at home and still claim under this policy. What other daily activities is your mom not able to do for herself?"

Janet though about it for a minute. "Well, she can't handle stairs, so she can't clean upstairs, or do the laundry in the basement anymore. And she needs to be taken to appointments and shopping. The doctor says she's not safe to drive."

"Right now, she's still reasonably independent, so she wouldn't quite qualify to claim. As she gets older, though, and needs more help she would. The policy is designed to provide the kind of care one gets in a long-term care facility to help with either deteriorated cognitive function or compromised activities of daily living (bathing, dressing, toileting, transfer from bed to bath, or standby assistance for bathing and transfer. Once there are at least two of these daily activities that she can't do herself, she can claim."

"Mom's sharp as a tack, but she needs more physical help every day. Last weekend she even asked me to help wash her hair because she can't lift her arms without pain....Wow. This makes a huge difference. She won't have to move to a nursing home. She'll be so relieved. Sally, you've made my day! I can't wait to tell my mom."

Sally throat tightened a little as she saw the joy on Janet's face. She had clearly been very worried about her mother's situation and Sally was delighted to help put her mind at ease. Before Sally could transition the conversation to the Tanwir's own roadmap, Wasai pre-empted her.

"This is great news for Elizabeth. Now I'm wondering—how are we doing? Do you have good news or bad news for us?"

"You don't waste any time, do you? Definitely good news."

Sally walked them through her recommendations and rationale, answering questions as they went along. Showing them their budget numbers[7] and her calculations for the various scenarios, she explained that their retirement income would cover their lifestyle expenses as well as her recommended savings and risk management strategies for the most part. The only scenario that left them a little short was full implementation of the roadmap combined with early retirement for Janet. As expected, they were a little shocked at Sally's recommendation to stop contributing to RRSPs in favour of other strategies, but seemed comfortable with the idea of relying on their pensions as the main source of table retirement income. She showed them that their pensions would provide a two-thirds survivor benefit and explained that most people experienced lower expenses after the death of a spouse, so this would likely be sufficient. Still, she had included a small joint life insurance policy as a cushion, just in case.

Wasai wanted to know more about Tax Free Savings Accounts, especially when Sally explained how they could supplement retirement income without attracting additional taxes. Janet was excited to find out grandparents could contribute to Registered Education Savings Plans, although she didn't think they needed to put in as much as Sally had

---

[7] A summary of expenses for the current and proposed scenarios for Wasai and Janet is provided at the end of this chapter.

earmarked, since Sara and Ali would surely set up RESPs as well.

Given their concerns about burdening each other and family in their later years, both Janet and Wasai appreciated the value of critical illness and long-term care insurance. The earlier conversation about Elizabeth's surprise policy certainly reinforced this. Sally also spent some time explaining the difference between temporary and permanent insurance, drawing attention to the fact that the premiums for Wasai's current Term 5 insurance would increase dramatically (3-4 times) in two years, and that the policy itself would terminate in seven years. The one redeeming feature of his policy was that he could convert it to permanent insurance before age 65 without medical underwriting. As she explained her risk management recommendations, Sally waited for the pushback she was expecting from Wasai. She was surprised when, instead, his main concern was his own insurability. Assuming he was referring to his age, she sought confirmation.

"The coverage and premiums I've proposed take your age and general health into account."

"Yes, but what about my condition? My blood tends to clot, so I have to take Coumadin every day."

"Ah. This is new information. If this is a permanent condition, you're right. Some of what I've suggested won't be possible. Either unavailable or just too expensive."

Wasai looked sheepish. "I should have told you. I was saving it as a reason to reject any insurance suggestions. Sorry."

Sally shook her head. "No need. And you don't need a pretext to reject anything I recommend. If you don't believe a strategy will do what you want it to, just say so. For now, let's finish reviewing the full roadmap to make sure you're comfortable with everything. Then I'll take this new information and any concerns you have back with me and prepare a 'plan B'."

The final section of the roadmap was estate planning. Janet and Wasai nodded as Sally described her recommendations for updating the wills and Powers of Attorney. She confirmed that the lawyer they used twelve years ago was still practicing and they were comfortable with him and urged them to making an appointment in the near future.

Sally then reviewed the potential tax implications for the estate and the fact that they would diminish over time as they used their assets to supplement their retirement income. After a brief discussion, Janet and Wasai agreed that Ali would be fine with the after-tax value of the estate. He was already doing quite well on his own and it didn't make sense to take out additional insurance just to save the taxes. If the tax bill was high, it would mean there were RRSPs and TFSAs left to pay it. If those assets were all gone, the tax bill would be minimal. Having said that, they both felt that a small policy to cover funeral costs and probate fees would make sense since Ali might not have cash available to cover those costs. Sally jotted down their preferences. Before she could move on to her last recommendation, the estate equalization strategy, Janet jumped in.

"What about Sara? You said you had an idea how we could leave something to her without putting her in the will."

Sally glanced over at Wasai to gauge his reaction before responding. He looked surprisingly at ease with Janet's question.

"That's the last thing we need to talk about today. I'm suggesting that you prepare your wills with Ali as executor and no mention of Sara, and then put a life insurance policy in place with Sara as beneficiary. The policy would pay out only after both of you die. You could leave the policy with Sara (or with your lawyer with instructions to convey it to Sara at that time). The proceeds of the policy would be tax free and would bypass the estate. Ali would never know unless you tell him. Hopefully, over the next few years, you'll find a way to bring your family back together. When that happens, you can revise your wills and cancel the policy if you want to."

Janet looked at Sally and then at her husband. "It would make me feel so much better to know both our babies and their babies will be looked after when we're gone."

Wasai nodded, stood up abruptly, and escaped to the bathroom.

Janet sighed. "He does that when he gets emotional. I called Sara the other day. Wasai agreed to listen in, as long as Sara didn't know he was there. At the end, she said what she always says 'Tell Dad I love him.' Wasai took off for the bathroom then too. He misses her so much. We really have to fix this."

"It sounds like you're making progress with Wasai. What about Ali?"

"I can't tackle Ali yet. I couldn't bear it if he pulled way from us."

They turned toward Wasai as he came back to the kitchen table. Sally started gathering her papers and asked if there were any more questions. Once again, Wasai surprised her.

"How do we get started? I know there are some things you still have to figure out, but I'd like to start working on the parts we agree with."

Sally thought about what they could work on before confirming the missing information. "Janet, what are your thoughts on when you'll retire?"

"Let's assume I'll work through to 65. If things work out better than expected, I can always retire earlier."

"On that basis, we could start the paperwork on a number of things" Sally wrote in her notebook as she listed out loud,

- "The applications for TFSAs and RESPs;

- estate equalization insurance—if you're comfortable with the $500,000 face value;

- small individual life insurance policies to provide some income top-up if one of you is left alone – I was planning to make this a joint policy, but with Wasai's condition, we'll have to covert his existing policy to avoid the medical and then put a separate policy in place for Janet;

- the small joint "last-to-die" policy that would cover probate and funeral costs in your final estate;

- and the critical illness and long-term care insurance for Janet.

I need to do a little more work on Wasai's situation to see what options are available for long-term care and critical illness coverage given the circumstances."

Janet looked at Wasai. "What do you think?"

"You're sure we can afford this?"

"The budget numbers say we can. I'd rather save more, help the kids, and take care of each other as we grow old than buy another water softener we don't need!"

They spent the next 30 minutes answering questions and filling out application forms. They completed the paperwork for the TFSAs first.

"Just to clarify:" Sally began as she put the first two signed applications aside, "we can only make a start on the RESP since it can't be fully set up until the baby is born and we have a social insurance number. Ali and Fariah also have to agree."

"They'll agree. They're convinced the child will be a genius with multiple degrees!"

Wasai snorted, "And save the world on weekends!"

Sally left the question of whether an RESP would be set up for Sara's baby for another day. There was no rush. Even so, she made a mental note to keep enough for both in the revised budget. Together they completed what they could on the one RESP application before moving on to the insurance policies. By the time they were done, they had completed applications for the following:

Critical illness and long-term care insurance and an individual life insurance policy for $100,000 on Janet; a joint $100,000 permanent policy that would pay out to the estate when they were both gone; as well as the $500,000 estate equalization policy (also permanent insurance), payable to Sara after they both passed on.

As they completed the paperwork, Sally explained the differences between term and permanent insurance[8] and pointed out the relevant clauses in each of the policies. She made a note to investigate the conversion option on Wasai's policy and find out what was required to convert the policy to a permanent one. As Sally described each item, Wasai was pleased to hear that the critical illness policy for Janet included a "return of premium" provision and Janet felt the $2,500 tax free benefit provided by the long-term care policy would be a godsend in her later years, when she would most likely be on her own.

Sally also made a point of explaining the underwriting process. While

---

[8] Gail Vaz-Oxlade offers a straight forward explanation of the main differences here http://www.gailvazoxlade.com/articles/just_in_case/term_vs_permanent_insurance.ht ml Including the following analogy: "If term insurance is rent, then permanent insurance is a mortgage payment; in the early years there isn't a lot of asset accumulation, but over the long term the pot will grow nicely."

certain policies were small enough to qualify for simplified underwriting and would proceed based on the applications they had just completed, others would require additional medical underwriting. She walked them through what that would involve and encouraged them to ask questions.

By the time they were done, they were more than ready to call it a day. Putting everything into a folder and sliding it into her satchel, Sally sat back. "Any more questions before I leave you to enjoy what's left of this lovely afternoon?"

Janet looked at Wasai and then back at Sally. "I think you've answered everything. What about you, Wasai?"

"No. But I might think of more later."

"That's fine. Any questions at all, you give me a call or email me. And I'll get back to you with answers about Wasai's insurance in the next day or two."

All three stood up at the same time and moved to the front door. Sally impulsively gave them both a quick hug and stepped out onto the porch. The last thing she saw, as she turned to wave goodbye, was Janet and Wasai framed in the storm door and surrounded by lilacs, with Vegas sitting at attention behind them on the hall table.

INCOME NEEDS NOW AND AT RETIREMENT

INCOME NEEDS - CURRENT SITUATION

INCOME (GROSS)	Wasai fully retired at 65		Janet retires at 60		Janet retires at 65	
	Janet	Wasai	Janet	Wasai	Janet	Wasai
Employment income (Janet)	$ 79,000.00	$ -	$ -	$ -	$ -	$ -
Pension income*	0	$ 22,100.00	$27,360.00	$23,807.00	$36,970.00	$ 25,648.00
CPP**	0	$ 5,280.00	$ 6,600.00	$ 5,544.00	$10,200.00	$ 5,832.00
OAS**	0	$ 6,960.00	0	$ 7,164.00	$ 7,536.00	$ 7,536.00
Rental Income (net of expenses)***	$ 6,750.00	$ 6,750.00	$ -	$ -	$ -	$ -
Taxable income from Investments****	$ -	$ -	$ 3,300.00	$ 3,300.00	$ 3,300.00	$ 3,300.00
Non taxable income from TFSA****			$ 1,500.00	$ 1,500.00	$ 1,500.00	$ 1,500.00
RRIF/Annuity income	$ -	$ -	$ 2,400.00	$ 3,000.00	$ 2,400.00	$ 3,000.00
Total Gross Income	$ 85,750.00	$ 41,090.00	$41,160.00	$44,315.00	$61,906.00	$ 46,816.00
Estimated income tax	$ 19,722.50	$ 4,519.90	$ 4,774.56	$ 3,899.72	$ 9,595.43	$ 4,541.15
Net Income	$ 66,027.50	$ 36,570.10	$36,385.44	$40,415.28	$52,310.57	$ 42,274.85
Monthly	$ 5,502.29	$ 3,047.51	$ 3,032.12	$ 3,367.94	$ 4,359.21	$ 3,522.90
COMBINED NET MONTHLY INCOME		$ 8,549.80		$ 6,400.06		$ 7,882.12
REQUIRED MONTHLY INCOME*****		$ 4,628.82		$ 4,986.55		$ 5,371.93
SURPLUS/SHORTFALL		$ 3,920.98		$ 1,413.51		$ 2,510.19

Assumptions

*Pension income is indexed for inflation at 1.5%

**CPP & OAS increase at 1% per year (once payments start)

***rental property is sold at Janet's retirement (current value assumed)

**** Projected income on investments of 3% annually

*****Retirement income needs indexed at 1.5% per year

INCOME NEEDS - WITH ALL ROADMAP RECOMMENDATIONS

INCOME (GROSS)	Wasai fully retired at 65		Janet retires at 60		Janet retires at 65	
	Janet	Wasai	Janet	Wasai	Janet	Wasai
Employment income (Janet)	$79,000.00	$ -	$ -	$ -	$ -	$ -
Pension income*	0	$ 22,100.00	$27,360.00	$23,807.00	$36,970.00	$25,648.00
CPP**	0	$ 5,280.00	$ 6,600.00	$ 5,544.00	$10,200.00	$ 5,832.00
OAS**	0	$ 6,960.00	0	$ 7,164.00	$ 7,536.00	$ 7,536.00
Rental Income (net of expenses)***	$ 6,750.00	$ 6,750.00	$ -	$ -	$ -	$ -
Taxable income from Investments****	$ -	$ -	$ 3,300.00	$ 3,300.00	$ 3,300.00	$ 3,300.00
Non taxable income from TFSA****			$ 1,500.00	$ 1,500.00	$ 1,500.00	$ 1,500.00
RRIF/Annuity income	$ -	$ -	$ 2,400.00	$ 3,000.00	$ 2,400.00	$ 3,000.00
Total Gross Income	$85,750.00	$41,090.00	$41,160.00	$44,315.00	$61,906.00	$46,816.00
Estimated income tax	$19,722.50	$ 4,519.90	$ 4,774.56	$ 3,899.72	$ 9,595.43	$ 4,541.15
Net Income	$66,027.50	$36,570.10	$36,385.44	$40,415.28	$52,310.57	$42,274.85
Monthly	$ 5,502.29	$ 3,047.51	$ 3,032.12	$ 3,367.94	$ 4,359.21	$ 3,522.90
COMBINED NET MONTHLY INCOME		$ 8,549.80		$ 6,400.06		$ 7,882.12
REQUIRED MONTHLY INCOME*****		$ 6,363.17		$ 6,856.95		$ 7,183.88
SURPLUS/SHORTFALL		$ 2,186.63		-$ 456.89		$ 698.24

Assumptions

*Pension income is indexed for inflation at 1.5%

**CPP & OAS increase at 1% per year (once payments start)

***rental property is sold at Janet's retirement (current value assumed)

**** Projected income on investments of 3% annually

*****Retirement income needs indexed at 1.5% per year (less fixed expenses)

Note: Reducing the Estate Equalization policy to $250,000 would allow Janet to retire at 60 with a slight surplus

KEY TAKEAWAYS

FOR CLIENTS

1. **Own it:** Your financial advisor can crunch the numbers, make recommendations and explain financial products, but nothing can happen unless you own your unique challenges and your chosen solutions. You make the final decisions. And, if there are personal roadblocks obstructing your journey, you have to own them too.

2. **Take it one step at a time:** Whether your goal is financial security or healing a broken relationship, be patient. These things take time. Make what progress you can, as you can. In the words of Max Ehrmann, "Beyond a wholesome discipline, be gentle with yourself."[9]

FOR ADVISORS

3. **Remember self-care:** Many financial advisors become emotionally invested in their clients. Hours spent discussing a client's most fundamental financial, health and personal challenges can foster strong attachments—it can also be exhausting! Especially when something difficult comes up that you can't resolve or overcome. It's important to recharge, refresh and take care of your own well-being. You can't be a resource for anyone if you're burnt out!

4. **Give people time:** These decisions can't be rushed. Take time to explain and answer questions thoroughly. Give your clients all the time they need to process the information you have provided.

5. **Always have a plan B:** At least one "elephant in the room" is a given in any kind of consultative relationship. There will always be something that everyone in the room (or everyone except the financial advisor!) knows, but no one is willing to talk about. It's not uncommon to discover the elephant just in time for it to step on and squash your best laid plans. Be prepared for the unexpected. Understand the available option. Always have a plan B.

---

[9] Max Ehrmann, excerpt from Desiderata, Copyright 1952

Notes and Questions

Notes and Questions

Notes and Questions

9. RESPONDING TO "WHAT IFS"

On the drive back to the office, Sally thought about the changes she would make to the Tanwir's roadmap. She was pleasantly surprised that both Janet and Wasai had focused on the benefits of the various solutions, rather than cost, especially given Wasai's earlier reluctance. Of course, it was a shame that Wasai's condition would prevent them from purchasing any new life, critical illness or long-term care insurance for him. His situation perfectly illustrated one of the great ironies of insurance: by the time one appreciates its value, it is often too late (or too expensive) to get coverage. One of Sally's greatest professional challenges was somehow encouraging younger people, with families and futures to protect, to understand this. Fortunately, Wasai's Term 5 insurance did have a conversion clause, so at least they would be able to provide the small amount of permanent life insurance he needed, without facing the obstacle of medical underwriting. Janet's excellent health and age would work in her favour—statistically speaking, she would most likely outlive Wasai by a significant margin and would benefit greatly from the long-term care and critical illness coverage. If she proved to be one of the lucky few who never experience a significant illness in their later years, the premiums paid for that coverage would be refunded to her estate for to benefit her heirs.

Everything was still rolling around in her head as she locked her car and walked into the office. Her eyes landed on the stack of mail on the reception desk, which reminded her, Lai Yee would be starting on Monday and it was already Thursday afternoon. If she finished up the Tanwir's changes tonight; tomorrow she could focus on preparing to onboard Lai Yee. If necessary, she could block off some time over the weekend too. Grabbing a coffee from the half-empty carafe in the lunchroom, Sally did a quick round of the office to touch base with everyone before settling in front of her computer.

Unlike Sally, Wasai and Janet had put the afternoon's conversation aside and were enjoying a coffee in the quiet and late afternoon sun of the back garden. Sitting in companionable silence, they breathed in the scent of spring blossoms and sun-warmed air. Janet listened to recently hatched robins chirping in chorus as the parent birds took turns satisfying their voracious offspring. Wasai suddenly reached out to touch her shoulder, and whispered, "Look."

Janet glanced in the direction he was pointing. The crab apple tree by the fence was a riot of pink-tinged creamy blossoms. "Yes, it's beautiful."

"No, look." Wasai whispered again and pointed.

Janet looked closer and noticed a flash of colour dancing around the crab apple tree. Moving slowly, she stood up and crept closer, Wasai right behind her. Two jewel-like hummingbirds hovered and darted from blossom to blossom; sunlight glinting off iridescent feathers. Hardly daring to breathe, Janet reached for Wasai's hand, pulling him to a stop a few feet from the tree. In the golden silence, they heard the hum of invisible wings as they gazed in fascination.

"Incredible," Janet sighed, "so much beauty and energy in such a small package. Makes me believe anything is possible."

Together they watched until the hummingbirds flitted away in their never-ending search for nectar. Reluctant to lose the sense of wonderment, they stood quietly for a few moments before returning to their abandoned coffee cups. In unison, they began clearing away the evidence of their late afternoon idyll.

"We'll have to head out soon. It takes about half an hour to get to the restaurant. We shouldn't keep them waiting."

"Hah. When are they ever on time!"

"Be nice." Janet stepped into the kitchen. "You can't expect Fariah to rush in her condition."

"I know. But it means we have lots of time." Wasai closed the patio door, put his coffee mug on the counter and grinned. "I can see how the game is going."

"Just don't get sucked into it. I know what you're like when you start watching soccer!" While Janet loaded the dishes into the dishwasher, Wasai headed to the living room, where the sound of cheering crowds and an enthusiastic sports announcer soon filled the room. Janet knew he would willingly turn off the television as soon as she was ready to go. He loved a good game of soccer or hockey, but he wasn't a fanatic. And he loved these bi-weekly dinners with Ali and Fariah as much as she did.

Thinking about their meeting with Sally that afternoon, and the magical encounter with the hummingbirds afterwards, Janet had a good feeling about things. Tonight, they would share the basics of their new financial roadmap with Ali and Fariah. Although she knew they would still hold back certain information, for the first time in a long time, Janet believed everything would work out and her family would soon be whole again.

In the meantime, while Wasai was focused on soccer, Janet decided to call her mother and let her know about that old insurance policy. After all, good feelings were meant to be shared.

*****

The following Thursday evening, as Sally reached for the doorbell, Wasai opened the door with Vegas in his arms. "Come in. Come in. Before the mosquitoes get you!"

"How did you know I was here? I just stepped up to the door!"

"Vegas recognizes the sound of your car. He comes out of hiding and waits by the door when you pull into the driveway. He's better than the doorbell."

Sally laughed and scratched Vegas between the ears. "This is the first time I've seen your house at night. The lights shining through the front windows look so welcoming. And that carriage lamp by the front door is lovely."

"Janet picked it up at some flea market years ago. She likes old brass."

As if on cue, Janet stepped into the hall from the kitchen, "Probably why I like you! Hi Sally. Thanks for agreeing to meet this late. I've used up all my personal days at work, so no more afternoon meetings for a while."

"No worries. I keep Tuesday and Thursday nights for evening meetings. Lots of clients have trouble fitting me in during the day."

As usual, they moved into the kitchen. "I made us something special today—Chai. Sort of a celebration."

"That's what smells so good." Sally looked at the steaming saucepan on the stove. "Did you make traditional Chai? Sweet, with lots of milk? Yum! What are we celebrating?"

Janet glanced at Wasai, who looked uncomfortable, but pleased. "Sara will be in Toronto next week for a conference. We're going to meet her for lunch on Saturday, before she flies out."

"Both of you? That's definitely worth celebrating!" Sally picked up a mug and held it high. "I'll drink to that!"

They sat down at the table, cradling steaming mugs of fragrant chai. For a moment, no one spoke, as they savoured the spicy brew and thought about life's strange twists. Janet was the first to break the silence. "I guess we should get down to business or we'll be here all night. Last week we told Ali and Fariah about our plans. Ali's glad we're updating the wills and proud to be our executor. They both appreciate our plans to set up an RESP for the baby. Ali wasn't familiar with critical illness or long-term care insurance. At first, he thought it made no sense to spend money on it. But, when I explained how my mom's policy would make such a difference for her, and for us, he came around. Of course, we didn't mention the policy for Sara." She glanced fondly at Wasai. "One breakthrough at a time."

Wasai snorted. "Breakthrough! Don't count your chickens...We don't know what will happen. For all you know, Sara wants to spit in my face!"

"Don't be ridiculous! Sara misses you as much as you miss her. When you see her, just hold her and give her a kiss. It will be fine."

Sally shook her head in mock distress. "You two. I don't know whether to hug you or shake you! While I figure that out—is there any Chai left?"

Her cup replenished, Sally pulled out their file. "Honestly, I'm so thrilled for you about Sara. Please let me know how it goes. Maybe we can eliminate the estate policy sooner than we thought."

"Hmm. I don't know. Wasai and Sara are marshmallows. Ali's more like a hazelnut. Sweet inside, but covered in a thick shell that's very hard to crack. It will take time."

"Fair enough. One step at a time, then. Let's focus on what we can do today."

Sally opened her file and started at the top. First, she presented the new $100,000 permanent life insurance policy for Janet. On the smaller policy, Janet qualified for simplified underwriting, so it had been issued almost immediately. Sally walked them through the policy, noting that Wasai was listed as beneficiary and explaining that the premiums would stay the same throughout her life. She described how the policy would gradually accumulate cash value, increasing the death benefit, and that this additional cash value could be accessed in an emergency through a policy loan.

When there were no more questions, Sally went on to confirm their suspicions about Wasai's insurability. He would not be eligible for any new insurance at reasonable rates. Certain companies would insure almost anyone, but, with his condition, the premiums would be out of reach. For Wasai, they would be better off putting aside some extra savings to deal with unexpected medical and care expenses.

Fortunately, she had confirmed that his existing Term 5 policy could be converted into the same kind of policy they had just reviewed for Janet. Sally had obtained the necessary paperwork from the issuer. She had also requested an estimate of premium at the next increase (in two years) for the Term 5 policy. Wasai and Janet were shocked to see it would increase to $702, when Wasai turned 65.

Sally recommended they convert the policy to a permanent policy, like the one they had just purchased for Janet, with the same $100,000 face value. Because of the conversion clause, Wasai would not need medical underwriting, but his age was still a factor. The permanent policy would have a fixed premium of $432 per month for life, but, unlike his current policy, the coverage would not expire at 70.

After a brief side conversation with Janet, Wasai reached for the paperwork, signed it and handed it back to Sally.

Next, they spent some time reviewing the revised budget. Sally had prepared three versions:

- one with the Term 5 policy continuing, including the increased premium in two years;

- one with the Term 5 policy cancelled outright; and

- one with the Term 5 policy converted to a $100,000 permanent policy.

They spent the most time reviewing the last of the three options, since it was Sally's recommended course of action.

INCOME (GROSS)	INCOME NEEDS - WITH ROADMAP AS IMPLEMENTED					
	Wasai fully retired at 65		Janet retires at 60		Janet retires at 65	
	Janet	Wasai	Janet	Wasai	Janet	Wasai
Employment income (Janet)	$79,000.00	$ -	$ -	$ -	$ -	$ -
Pension income*	0	$22,100.00	$27,360.00	$23,807.00	$36,970.00	$25,648.00
CPP**	0	$ 5,280.00	$ 6,600.00	$ 5,544.00	$10,200.00	$ 5,832.00
OAS**	0	$ 6,960.00	0	$ 7,164.00	$ 7,536.00	$ 7,536.00
Rental Income (net of expenses)***	$ 6,750.00	$ 6,750.00	$ -	$ -	$ -	$ -
Taxable income from Investments***	$ -	$ -	$ 3,300.00	$ 3,300.00	$ 3,300.00	$ 3,300.00
Non taxable income from TFSA****			$ 1,500.00	$ 1,500.00	$ 1,500.00	$ 1,500.00
RRIF/Annuity income	$ -	$ -	$ 2,400.00	$ 3,000.00	$ 2,400.00	$ 3,000.00
Total Gross Income	$85,750.00	$41,090.00	$41,160.00	$44,315.00	$61,906.00	$46,816.00
Estimated income tax	$19,722.50	$ 4,519.90	$ 4,774.56	$ 3,899.72	$ 9,595.43	$ 4,541.15
Net Income	$66,027.50	$36,570.10	$36,385.44	$40,415.28	$52,310.57	$42,274.85
Monthly	$ 5,502.29	$ 3,047.51	$ 3,032.12	$ 3,367.94	$ 4,359.21	$ 3,522.90
COMBINED NET MONTHLY INCOME		$ 8,549.80		$ 6,400.06		$ 7,882.12
REQUIRED MONTHLY INCOME*****		$ 5,959.43		$ 6,247.46		$ 6,557.74
SURPLUS/SHORTFALL		$ 2,590.37		$ 152.60		$ 1,324.38

Assumptions
*Pension income is indexed for inflation at 1.5%
**CPP & OAS increase at 1% per year (once payments start)
***rental property is sold at Janet's retirement (current value assumed)
**** Projected income on investments of 3% annually
*****Retirement income needs indexed at 1.5% per year (less fixed expenses)

As they reviewed the third version of the revised budget, Sally pointed out that she had included a $1,000 per year RESP contribution for each of two anticipated grandchildren, although they had only mentioned Ali's expected baby in their last meeting. Janet and Wasai nodded in agreement. Sally also drew their attention to an increased surplus, since she had removed the premiums for long-term care and critical illness insurance for Wasai. In fact, based on the revised budget, even if Janet retired at 60, they would have a small surplus.

Janet was pleased, but felt she would still plan to retire at 65, to be on the safe side. Sally agreed and suggested, given the surplus, that they increase their savings and reduce the amount of income being drawn from savings at retirement. This would allow them to build up more of an emergency buffer.

Then Sally did something she hadn't done at any of their previous meetings: she pulled out her notebook computer and logged in. "I want to show you how you can check on your TFSA accounts. Do you have Wi-Fi?"

"Yes. Look for Tanwir. The password is Vegas"

Hearing his name, Vegas appeared at the kitchen door. Purring, he rubbed against Sally's ankles on his way to Wasai's lap. "Silly cat." Wasai reached behind him to the counter and grabbed a small bag of cat treats.

Sally turned the computer around so Wasai and Janet could see the screen. She showed them how to switch between their accounts and where to find a summary, individual transactions and periodic statements. "Once we have the RESP's set up, you'll be able to check them online too. Any other savings or investments you have with me will also be accessible here. I've written down the instructions here, including the temporary password. Change it to something you'll remember. But make it harder to guess than Vegas!"

Wasai clicked through the various screens for a few more minutes, with Janet looking over his shoulder, before turning the notebook back to Sally. "I like this. Being able to check whenever I want to."

"You won't see a lot of change. Just slow growth until you start drawing out the income, and then it will stay the same. We're focused on preserving your capital and generating predictable income—no volatile investments for you!"

"Good. The last thing I need is Wasai following stocks and stressing me out every time our account balance changes!"

Wasai opened his mouth to respond, but thought better of it and muttered something in Vegas' ear instead.

Closing the computer, Sally went back to her notes, checking off items on a list. She asked whether they had been contacted by the medical underwriter for the $500,000 estate equalization policy, as well as Janet's critical illness and long-term care policies. Janet confirmed she had made the necessary appointments. Wasai had organized things with the lawyer, who they would meet with next month. Everything was moving along as it should.

Sally closed her file. "Are there any more revelations before we call it a night?"

Laughing, Janet reached over and put her hand on Wasai's shoulder. "No, I think we're 'surprised out' for now."

Wasai nodded, slowly stroking the cat. "I envy Vegas. He doesn't have to think. He eats treats, watches birds, gets stroked and lies in the sun. No wonder he purrs."

"So true—if only life were so simple! It's getting late and I know you'd like to relax and enjoy the rest of your evening."

They pushed back from the table and stood up. Vegas slid off Wasai's lap and sauntered into the hallway.

"Before I head out, there are a couple final things to cover. First, it has been a real pleasure getting to know you. Thank you for welcoming me into your home and for placing your trust in me. I am truly honoured."

Wasai and Janet looked pleased and a little embarrassed.

"You're welcome Sally. Thanks for being patient with us – especially Wasai!" Janet nudged her husband.

"Haha, very funny!" Wasai glanced over at Sally and spoke softly. "You're easy to talk to. And Vegas likes you."

Sally laughed. "And I like Vegas! I also want you to know we'll continue to meet regularly over the next few months as we put everything in place. This roadmap isn't cast in stone. If something significant changes in your life, we'll reassess and make any necessary changes. Even once everything's set up, we'll connect every six months or so, and any time something changes or you have questions. I'm always available by phone or email. And remember, my team is there for you too."

"Thank you. That's good to know."

"It's strange. A few months ago, we were unsure about everything. Now, it feels like we know exactly where we're going."

"I'm even starting to believe our family can become whole again, along the way."

Sally drew them into a warm hug. "I am convinced of it!"

Notes and Questions

Notes and Questions

Notes and Questions

10. CONCLUSION: THE WAY FORWARD

When we met Wasai and Janet Tanwir, they had no clear plan for reaching their financial and personal goals. In fact, they hadn't taken the time to identify any! This was largely because they didn't think in those terms. Like most people, they were focused on going to work, taking care of their home and family, and living their life from day to day.

Of course, it is also likely they avoided thinking about some things, like wills and legacies, because doing so would mean facing up to the chasm their daughter's sexuality had triggered within the family. It wasn't until a close friend faced the reality of living alone and supporting herself after the loss of her husband that the Tanwir's suddenly looked mortality in the face. John's death was their wake-up call. It made them realize that leaving things to chance could be dangerous and it was time to make a plan.

Fortunately, as naturally prudent and conscientious people, they had made many good decisions over the years. Despite this, to a great extent, their relative financial security was more luck than intent. At any point in their lives together, one significant tragedy could have brought about devastating financial consequences; just as Sara's unexpected announcement wrought emotional havoc within their unsuspecting, conservative family.

As it stands, with two incomes, a rental property and a modest lifestyle, Wasai and Janet have good cash flow and a few more years to build on what they have done do far. They also have the advantage of employer pensions to help them in their retirement years. More importantly, with the roadmap Sally has helped them put in place, they now have the space to sort through their family complications. At the same time, they can now:

- bolster retirement savings with some tax-free retirement income;

- leave a legacy to their children and grandchildren (even after the obligatory probate fees and tax grab!);

- provide for their own care in the event of a life-changing illness or the need for long-term care; and

- even put aside something extra so they can travel once or twice a year when they retire.

As a bonus, having access to Sally's expertise allowed them to sort out some of Janet's mother's finances. This lifted a huge burden from Janet's shoulders. She had been watching her mother struggle to stay independent and worried what the future would hold as her mom needed more and more support. Now she knows that resources are available to pay for some extra care so her mother doesn't have to feel like a burden as she ages and Janet doesn't have to worry about not being there for her as much as she would like to.

While Janet and Wasai are not "real", the challenges they faced and the complexities they struggled with are actual scenarios I have encountered in my practice. The strategies Sally put together for the Tanwirs are just a few of the many ways she could have responded to their unique circumstances, preferences and needs. It is also important that they know their options are not "cast in stone." As Sally explained earlier, a financial roadmap is a living document. It must be monitored and changed as needs and circumstances change. This will be especially relevant for Wasai and Janet, since they have embarked on a mission to mend the rift within their growing family.

I hope this story effectively illustrates what I consider to be one of the most fascinating elements of being a financial advisor: peeling back the layers to find the agony and aspiration that hides beneath the surface of everyone's financial questions. Because it's never really about the money. We all have a relationship with money (unhealthy or otherwise!), but the currency itself is just a tool that, when managed well, can help alleviate the agony and achieve the aspiration. A financial advisor is simply someone who has mastered the use of this essential tool and chosen to make a profession out of helping others use it better.

In truth, financial and insurance planning is about protection, caring for loved ones, avoiding calamity, ensuring balance and creating security. More often than not, the exploratory process of working with a good financial advisor uncovers feelings and assumptions that people seldom, if ever, talk about. They may not even know these feelings and assumptions exist. More importantly, along the way, the financial planning process helps people identify what truly matters; whether that involves helping family, maintaining personal health, retiring comfortably, leaving a legacy (to family, community, or a charity), or something else.

Here are just two examples of the impact good financial and insurance planning can have when life takes an unexpected turn for the worse.

Patricia A. Muir

Patricia is an executive consultant, coach, and advocate for best practices for great workplaces and "good" profits. This is her story:

In 2013, I was diagnosed with breast cancer. As a business owner, the logistical part of coping with my personal and professional challenges was easy: reschedule clients and adjust workload. However, the emotional drain directly jeopardized my ability to focus on my work and in order to heal physically and emotionally, I needed to adjust my pace and say "no" to work. Normally for most of us, this would have spelled financial disaster.

Fortunately, I had critical illness insurance. The policy paid out quickly and efficiently allowing me to focus on my Self-care immediately. Knowing that I had additional tax-free funds to see me through this crisis contributed greatly to my peace-of-mind and reduced my overall stress.

In a 2012 study conducted by Canadian Partnership Against Cancer, 60% of individuals with cancer reported a loss of income in the 12 months following diagnosis. Those who returned to work during their treatment or earlier than desirable, cited financial need as the reason. I am an avid promoter of critical illness insurance for its value in contributing to wellbeing and peace-of-mind at a time when most needed.

Following recovery from breast cancer, Patricia developed a signature program for women executives and entrepreneurs returning to work during or after cancer treatment. The program is based on emotional intelligence and leadership peak performance.

This next example comes from a family who, although preferring to remain anonymous, felt they had to share their experience. They were fortunate enough to meet a financial advisor shortly after immigrating to Canada and that one lucky encounter made such a difference.

A GRATEFUL IMMIGRANT

Our family arrived in Canada escaping from a life of terror, fear and war. We came with suitcases filled with hope desire and aspirations of living a normal life. A close family friend, a financial advisor, convinced my dad to purchase a simple insurance policy. She said, as we had no family here to support us, that having a policy was important.

My dad, reluctantly purchased the policy, not happy to be spending money that was meant for a rainy day. We were living in the basement of someone's home until my dad could find a job. My mom was a stay at home mom. Tough times.

Little did we know how much tougher life was about to get. My dad went to a job interview and on his way back home, suffered a heart attack and died. That insurance policy, so reluctantly purchased, allowed us to continue to live here, go to school and live our lives in a safe and caring environment.

I Cannot even imagine what would have happened if a wise and caring person had not offered guidance to my father, totally understanding the potential hardships of immigrants in an unknown environment

Of course, you may be thinking you don't have the kind of challenges Janet, Wasai and these other families struggle with. Maybe your life is less complicated than theirs and you just need to know how to reach your financial goals as quickly and efficiently as possible. Maybe the most taxing part of your life is simply that–taxes! Regardless, a financial advisor can help sort through the myriad of options available and help you define a strategy to achieve your specific objectives.

Interestingly enough, even if you are not looking for personal insights, you will likely gain some peace of mind from working with an advisor. In a recent survey conducted by Mackenzie Financial, 68% of Canadians who use a financial advisor feel confident about achieving their retirement goals compared to 38% of those who don't use an advisor.[10] Research has also found that Investors who work with advisors for 15 years or more accumulate 2.7 times more in savings than comparable investors without advice.[11] And, if you are a big picture kind of person, you'll be interested to know that the Conference Board of Canada states, if 10% more Canadian households chose to save with an advisor, overall household wealth [in Canada] would increase by $4.8 billion and our GDP would grow by an additional $2.3 billion over a 45-year period.[12]

With these startling statistics in mind, the following pages recap the key client takeaways from the story of Janet and Wasai Tanwir. More than anything, these tips will help you make the most of your financial journey and any advisor relationships you cultivate along the way.

Let's start with the key takeaways for clients and prospective clients: those who prefer to tap into third party expertise.

For Clients

Work with a financial advisor: It pays to find a good financial advisor – both in terms of improved financial circumstances and in greater peace of mind.

Ask a friend: One of the best ways to find a good financial advisor is by asking friends you trust and respect.

Ensure a good fit: The financial advisor you choose to work with represents a new, long-term relationship in your life. Find the right one.

Ask questions: At every stage of your relationship with a financial advisor, always ask the questions that occur to you. A good advisor loves questions.

---

[10] Mackenzie Financial Corporation, Confidence Boosters for Canadians Saving for Retirement, http://mackenz.ie/2e15hGD
[11] Claude Montmarquette and Nathalie Viennot-Briot, The Value of Financial Advice, The Annals of Economics and Finance, 16-1, pp. 69 – 94, 2015.
[12] 3 The Conference Board of Canada, Boosting Retirement Readiness and the Economy Through Financial Advice, September 2014.

Be open: Holding back or being less than honest with your advisor may expose you to unnecessary risk or result in a plan that is less than ideal.

Value the team: While it can be gratifying to have the undivided attention of one personal financial advisor, having a whole team on your side means better access, enhanced customer service, continuity of relationships, and deeper expertise.

Examine your relationship with money: Think about what money means to you and how you use and your financial journey will be more successful.

Be prepared: Take the time to pull together all the information your advisor asks for.

Know what matters: Throughout the financial planning process you will have to think seriously about what really matters to you and your family, even when those priorities differ.

Accept that families are complicated: While still the primary social unit in most societies around the world, there is no such thing as a simple family. Accept that and work with it.

Know yourself: As you design your financial roadmap, be sure the route and destination you choose truly reflects where you want to go and how you want to get there.

Accept support: No journey is made in complete solitude and no goal is accomplished entirely alone. There is no disgrace in asking for help and accepting support when it is offered.

Do the work: When you decide to put your financial house in order, be prepared to do the work—have the tough conversations, make the decisions and take action.

Own it: Your financial advisor can crunch the numbers, make recommendations and explain financial products, but nothing can happen unless you own your unique challenges and your chosen solutions.

Take it one step at a time: Be patient with yourself and each other. These things take time.

If you were reading this book from the perspective of a financial advisor, I hope the model illustrated by Sally resonates with you. In my experience, a relationship based, customer-centric practice is the most fulfilling and the most successful. As long as you stay focused on understanding your clients first, and then striving to build the best possible response to their unique needs and circumstances, you will create a win-win, positive spiral that benefits both your clients and your practice.

Here again are the key advisor takeaways from Sally's interactions with the Tanwirs and her team.

Be referable: Every financial advisor knows that the strongest practice is built on referrals. But referrals will only come if you are referable.

Be accessible: Even the best clients won't refer you if they think you are too busy to take on new clients. Make sure your clients know you like referrals.

Honour your clients' trust in you: Follow up on referrals and treat them like gold to honour your client's trust in you.

Earn trust: Every interaction with your client (or prospective client) is an opportunity to build trust. Remember to demonstrate: Intent, Commonality, Propriety and Capability in both words and actions.

Listen, listen, listen: Demonstrate that you care and make people feel valued and respected by listening actively and intently. Besides, you can't know your client without listening.

Ensure confidentiality: It is your responsibility to protect your clients' privacy. Remember to let your clients know you take confidentiality seriously and will always secure their information and respect their privacy.

Never assume: Inaccurate assumptions about what is normal or common in a particular demographic can be costly to your clients. Make sure you fully understand the real situation and that your client has all the information needed to make an informed decision.

Offer options: There is seldom one perfect solution to any financial challenge. Do your homework and distill the information available into a few good options.

SHEHNAZ HUSSAIN

No one knows everything: Expecting to know everything about every aspect of your clients' financial needs is unrealistic. Collaborate. Draw on your team or cultivate outside experts for information outside your area of expertise.

Welcome questions: Encourage your clients to ask questions. Never dismiss a question or treat it as trivial.

Be holistic: Approach each client with a spirit of discovery. Set out to understand the whole picture before jumping to solutions.

Offer clear guidance: Your clients come to you for a reason. They need guidance and clear explanations. Simplify financial complexity so they can move forward.

Encourage the exploration: Don't rush the process. Make it safe for your clients to join you on a personal voyage of discovery.

Accept that families are complicated: When you come to the table as a financial advisor, never underestimate the impact of family on the planning process and on the final decisions your client will make.

Keep learning: Good financial advisors are lifelong learners. Approach your practice and the people you serve with an open, enquiring mind and every moment will be a learning moment.

Expect emotion: Most of the topics you delve into will be fraught with emotion. You will learn more about your clients than their best friends. Expect it to get emotional.

Be (or become) sensitive: Because the topics you discuss with clients, as a financial advisor, are private, personal and emotionally-laden, sensitivity and emotional intelligence are critical assets.

Remember self-care: It's important to recharge, refresh and take care of your own well-being. You can't be a resource for your clients or your loved-ones if you're burnt out.

Give people time: Give clients time to process the information you provide and take time to explain things thoroughly. Don't rush things.

Always have a plan B: There will always be something that everyone in the room (or everyone except the financial advisor!) knows, but no one talks about. Be prepared for the unexpected. Always have a plan B.

Inevitably, even after reading this book, some people will prefer to manage their finances without the help of an advisor. Perhaps this includes you. Maybe you have a financial industry background and are uniquely qualified; or maybe you enjoy self-educating and staying current with the ever-changing financial landscape.

For those readers who fall into the do-it-yourself category, you will find some downloadable tools and checklists in electronic form at www.whathappensifbook.com.

Whichever route you choose to follow toward financial success and security—and the peace of mind that comes with them—may the journey be informative, enlightening and, above all, rewarding.

Notes and Questions

GLOSSARY

DPSP: A deferred profit sharing plan is a structure that allows an organization to put aside a portion of annual profits for the future benefit of employees.

POA: Power of Attorney documents allow you to appoint someone you trust to make financial and/or personal and healthcare decisions for you when you are unable to make those decisions on your own behalf.

RESP: A registered education savings plan allows parents and/or other interested parties to put aside money for the future education of a minor. These savings grow on a tax sheltered basis for the duration of the plan, although contributions are not tax-deductible. Currently, the Government of Canada matches eligible contributions to a maximum amount per child.

RRSP: A registered retirement savings plan allows eligible Canadians to make tax-deductible contributions to their personal retirement savings to an annual maximum amount based on their income in the previous year. Money invested in an RRSP grows tax-free until it is withdrawn, at which point withdrawals are included in taxable income of the recipient.

TFSA: A tax free savings account allows eligible Canadians to put aside additional savings up to the allowable annual maximum. Contributions to a TFSA are not tax-deductible, but the income and growth generated by the savings is tax-free, even at withdrawal.

More information about all of these programs is available on the Canada Revenue Agency website.

http://www.cra-arc.gc.ca/

Critical Illness Insurance: An insurance policy that provides a lump sum cash payment if the policyholder is diagnosed with one of the specific illnesses on a predetermined list. These policies may also be structured to pay out regular income in the event of critical illness. The payout may also be made in the event of the policyholder undergoing a specific surgical procedure; for example, a heart bypass operation.

Disability Insurance: An Insurance policy that provides a partial replacement of income, in the form of a disability benefit, when income is lost due to illness or injury. Most disability insurance policies pay a fixed sum, usually a percentage of regular income, for a fixed period of time. Other policies pay a monthly sum for the entire period the insured is disabled from earning suitable income, as determined by his or her qualifications, experience, and training.

Long-Term Care Insurance: An insurance policy covers all or some of the cost of nursing-home care, home-health care, personal or adult day care for individuals above the age of 65 or with a chronic or disabling condition that needs constant supervision.

Permanent Life Insurance: Permanent life insurance is an umbrella term for life insurance policies that don't expire and typically combine a death benefit with a savings component. The two main types of permanent life insurance are whole life and universal life insurance policies.

Term Insurance: Term insurance is a type of life insurance policy that provides coverage for a certain period of time, or a specified "term" of years. If the insured dies during the time period specified in the policy and the policy is active (in force), then a death benefit will be paid. Unlike permanent insurance, Term life insurance cannot be renewed beyond a certain age specified within the policy.

SOME QUESTIONS TO CONSIDER

What are your short, medium and long-term financial goals?

What financial situations keep you awake at night worrying?

Do you have enough net wealth to fund your life's goals? If not, how much more do you need?

Are you too indebted for comfort?

Are you paying too much in taxes?

Do you have a monthly budget? If so, do you have difficulty sticking to it?

Should you prioritize increasing assets, or paying down debts?

Are your financial assets well-diversified?

If something happened to you, how much would your family (dependents) need to survive and for how long?

Are you taking advantage of the Registered Education Savings Plans and the Canada Education Savings Grant?

When do you hope to retire?

What sorts of things do you hope to do when you retire?

What expenses do you expect will decrease or increase when you retire?

Do you think you might work part-time after retirement?

Have you named a beneficiary on all of your retirement accounts?

Will your family have enough to pay taxes on your estate?

Are you concerned about leaving money to your heirs, or do you want to exhaust your retirement funds completely?

Do you have real estate other than your home? If so, how will it be taxed when passed on. Will your heirs be able to keep it?

Have you created a will? Is it up to date?

Are multiple families or unusual family circumstances involved?

Are you concerned about equally distributing your assets between family members?

Are you aware of, or worried about, the probate fees your estate may face? What have you done to minimize them?

Are you leaving funds to any charities? If so, have you confirmed that you have the exact, correct name of the charities in question, to avoid any confusion about your bequest?

Do you have powers of attorney for property and personal care? If so, whom have you named as attorneys and contingents?

Have you made or considered making an advance health-care directive, or living will?

Does your executor and/or substitute decision maker know where to find important documents along with a list of your trusted advisors?

Do you own a business? If so, what will you do with it when you retire?

Who will own the business in the event of your death or disability?

Do you have a buy-sell agreement in place? If so, is it adequately funded by assets or insurance?

Is there sufficient liquidity in the business to sustain operations during a transition?

ABOUT THE AUTHOR

Shehnaz Hussain is the founder and CEO of Intuitive Financial Solutions, a Toronto based insurance company that helps individuals put their financial security on a solid foundation. A committed life-long learner, she holds a B.Sc., B.Ed., and H.Ed.. With over 15 years of experience in the insurance industry as a financial advisor and manager, Shehnaz is a Chartered Life Underwriter (CLU), a Certified Health Insurance Specialist (CHS) and an Elder Planning Counsellor (EPC).

The philosophy that Shehnaz brings to her practice has been greatly influenced by her own life – she was a caregiver for her mother at an early age, making her sensitive to the needs of vulnerable people. As a young woman, her work experience reinforced that belief and she realized that people need to be educated about the risks and challenges that life presents and the alternative solutions that are available.

Within her own company, Shehnaz fosters an inclusive and collaborative working environment, where everyone is focused on client needs, wants and realities. Together with her growing team, Shehnaz finds meaning and purpose in her work and in her life by protecting her clients from the "what IFS" in theirs.

Made in the USA
Charleston, SC
10 February 2017